# The Prisoner of
# Second Avenue

Lee Grant as EDNA EDISON and Peter Falk as MEL EDISON

# the Prisoner of Second Avenue

A NEW COMEDY BY

## Neil Simon

DIRECTED ON BROADWAY
BY MIKE NICHOLS

RANDOM HOUSE ⌂ NEW YORK

Photographs by courtesy of Martha Swope

THE PRISONER OF SECOND AVENUE *was first presented on November 11, 1971, by Saint-Subber at the Eugene O'Neill Theater, New York City, with the following cast:*

*(In order of appearance)*

| | |
|---|---|
| MEL EDISON | Peter Falk |
| EDNA EDISON | Lee Grant |
| HARRY EDISON | Vincent Gardenia |
| PEARL | Florence Stanley |
| JESSIE | Tresa Hughes |
| PAULINE | Dena Dietrich |

*Setting by* Richard Sylbert
*Lighting by* Tharon Musser
*Costumes by* Anthea Sylbert

## The Scene

*The entire action takes place in a Manhattan apartment, on Second Avenue in the upper eighties.*

## Act One

Scene One: Two-thirty in the morning on a midsummer's day.

Scene Two: Late afternoon, a few days later.

## Act Two

Scene One: Mid-September; about one in the afternoon.

Scene Two: Midafternoon, two weeks later.

Scene Three: A late afternoon in mid-December.

# ACT ONE

*The scene is a fourteenth-floor apartment in one of those prosaic new apartment houses that grow like mushrooms all over New York's overpriced East Side. This one is on Second Avenue in the upper eighties. The management calls this a five-and-a-half-room apartment. What is visible to us is the living room–dining room combination, a small, airless and windowless kitchen off the dining room, a French door that leads to a tiny balcony or terrace off the living room, and a small hallway that leads to two bedrooms and bathrooms.*

*This particular dwelling has been the home of* MEL *and* EDNA EDISON *for the past six years. What they thought they were getting was all the modern luxuries and comforts of the smart, chic East Side. What they got is paper-thin walls and a view of five taller buildings from their terrace.*

*The stage is dark. It is two-thirty in the morning and a hot midsummer's day has just begun.*

*It is silent . . .*

*In pajamas, robe and slippers,* MEL EDISON *sits alone on the tiny sofa, smoking a cigarette. He rubs his face anxiously, then coughs . . .*

MEL   Ohhh, Christ Almighty.

    *(A light goes on in the bedroom.* EDNA, *his wife, appears in her nightgown)*

EDNA   What's wrong?

MEL   Nothing's wrong.

EDNA   Huh?

MEL   Nothing's wrong. Go back to bed.

EDNA    Are you sure?

MEL    I'm sure. Go back to bed. (EDNA *turns and goes back into the bedroom*) Oh, God, God, God.
     (EDNA *returns, putting on her robe. She flips the switch on the wall, lighting the room*)

EDNA    What is it? Can't you sleep?

MEL    If I could sleep, would I be sitting here calling God at two-thirty in the morning?

EDNA    What's the matter?

MEL    Do you know it's twelve degrees in there? July twenty-third, the middle of a heat wave, it's twelve degrees in there.

EDNA    I told you, turn the air conditioner off.

MEL    And how do we breathe? (*Points to the window*) It's eighty-nine degrees out there . . . eighty-nine degrees outside, twelve degrees inside. Either way they're going to get me.

EDNA    We could leave the air conditioner on and open the window.
     (*She goes into the kitchen*)

MEL    They don't work that way. Once the hot air sees an open window, it goes in.

EDNA    We could leave the air conditioner off for an hour. Then when it starts to get hot, we can turn it back on.
     (*She comes out, eating from a jar of applesauce*)

MEL    Every hour? Seven times a night? That's a good idea. I can get eight minutes sleep in between working the air conditioner.

EDNA    *I'll* do it. *I'll* get up.

MEL  I asked you a million times to call that office. That air conditioner hasn't worked properly in two years.

EDNA  I called them. A man came. He couldn't find anything wrong.

MEL  What do you mean, nothing wrong? I got it on Low, it's twelve goddamned degrees.

EDNA  *(Sits down, sighing)* It's not twelve degrees, Mel. It's cold, but it's not twelve degrees.

MEL  All right, seventeen degrees. Twenty-nine degrees. Thirty-six degrees. It's not sixty-eight, sixty-nine. A temperature for a normal person.

EDNA  *(Sits on the sofa)*  I'll call them again tomorrow.

MEL  Why do they bother printing on it High, Medium and Low? It's all High. Low is High. Medium is High. Some night I'm gonna put it on High, they'll have to get a flamethrower to get us out in the morning.

EDNA  What do you want me to do, Mel? You want me to turn it off? You want me to leave it on? Just tell me what to do.

MEL  Go back to sleep.

EDNA  I can't sleep when you're tense like this.

MEL  I'm not tense. I'm frozen stiff. July twenty-third.
*(He sits down on the sofa)*

EDNA  You're tense. You were tense when you walked in the house tonight. You've been tense for a week. Would you rather sleep in here? I could make up the cot.

MEL  You can't even sit in here. *(Picks up the small puff pillows from behind him)* Why do you keep these ugly little pillows on here? You spend eight hundred dollars for chairs

and then you can't sit on it because you got ugly little pillows shoved up your back.
*(He throws one of the pillows on the floor)*

EDNA I'll take the pillows off.

MEL Edna, please go inside, I'll be in later.

EDNA It's not the air conditioner. It's not the pillows. It's something else. Something's bothering you. I've seen you when you get like this. What is it, Mel?

MEL *(Rubs his face with his hands)* It's nothing. I'm tired. *(He gets up and goes over to the terrace door)*

EDNA I'm up, Mel, you might as well tell me.

MEL It's nothing, I'm telling you . . . I don't know. It's everything. It's this apartment, it's this building, it's this city. Listen. Listen to this. *(He opens the terrace door. We hear the sounds of traffic, horns, motors, etc.)* Two-thirty in the morning, there's one car driving around in Jackson Heights and we can hear it . . . Fourteen stories up, I thought it would be quiet. I hear the subway up here better than I hear it in the subway . . . We're like some kind of goddamned antenna. All the sound goes up through this apartment and then out to the city.

EDNA We've lived here six years, it never bothered you before.

MEL It's worse now, I don't know why. I'm getting older, more sensitive to sounds, to noise. Everything. *(He closes the door, then looks at himself)* You see this? I had that door opened ten seconds, you gotta wash these pajamas now.

EDNA *(Anything to please)* Give them to me, I'll get you clean pajamas.

MEL *(Pacing)* Two-thirty in the morning, can you believe that's still going on next door?
*(He points to the wall)*

EDNA What's going on?

MEL What are you, trying to be funny? You mean to tell me you don't hear that?

EDNA *(Puzzled)* Hear what?

MEL *(Closer to the wall, still pointing)* That! That! What are you, deaf? You don't hear that?

EDNA Maybe I'm deaf. I don't hear anything.

MEL *Listen,* for God's sakes . . . You don't hear "Raindrops Falling on His Head"? *(He sings)* Da dum de dum da dum de da . . . "too big for his feet" . . . You don't hear that?

EDNA Not when you're singing, I don't hear it.

MEL *(Stares at the wall)* It's those two goddamned German airline hostesses. Every night they got someone else in there. Two basketball players, two hockey players, whatever team is in town, win or lose, they wind up in there . . . Every goddamned night! . . . Somewhere there's a 747 flying around with people serving themselves because those two broads never leave that apartment. *(He grabs* EDNA, *pulls her over to the wall)* Come here. You mean to tell me you don't hear that?

EDNA *(Puts her ear against the wall)* Yes, now I hear it.

MEL You see! Is it any wonder I don't sleep at night?

EDNA *(Moving away from the wall)* Don't sleep with your head next to the wall. Sleep in the bedroom.

MEL Hey, knock it off in there. It's two damn thirty in the lousy morning. *(He bangs on the wall, then stops and looks*

7

*at it. He points to the wall)* Look at that, I cracked the wall. I barely touched it, the damned thing is cracked.

EDNA   It was starting to crack before. There's a leak somewhere; one of the pipes upstairs is broken.

MEL   A two million-dollar building, you can't touch the walls? It's a good thing I didn't try to hang a picture; we all could have been killed.

EDNA   They know about it. They're starting to fix it on Monday.

MEL   *(He sits down)*   Not Monday. Tomorrow. I want that wall fixed tomorrow, it's a health hazard. And they're going to repaint the whole wall, and if it doesn't match, they'll paint the rest of the room, and if that doesn't match, they'll do the rest of the apartment. And I'm not paying for it, you understand?

EDNA   I'll tell them.

MEL   And tell them about the air conditioner . . . and the window in the bedroom that doesn't open except when it rains and then you can't shut it until there's a flood and then tell them about our toilet that never stops flushing.

EDNA   It stops flushing if you jiggle it.

MEL   Why should I have to jiggle it? For the money I'm paying here do I have to stand over a toilet in the middle of the night and have to jiggle every time I go to the bathroom?

EDNA   When you're through, get back into bed, tell me and *I'll* jiggle it.

MEL   *(Turns, glares at her)*   Go to bed, Edna. I don't want to talk to you now. Will you please go to sleep.

EDNA   I can't sleep if I know you're up here walking around having an anxiety attack.

MEL   I'm not having an anxiety attack. I'm a little tense.

EDNA   Why don't you take a Valium?

MEL   I took one.

EDNA   Then take another one.

MEL   I took another one. They don't work any more.
(*He sits down in a chair*)

EDNA   *Two* Valiums? They *have* to work.

MEL   They don't work any more, I'm telling you. They're supposed to calm you down, aren't they? All right, am I calm? They don't work. Probably don't put anything in them. Charge you fourteen dollars for the word "Valium." (*He bangs on the wall*) Don't you ever fly anywhere? Keep somebody in Europe awake!
(*He bangs on the wall again with his fist*)

EDNA   Stop it, Mel. You're really getting me nervous now. What's wrong? Has something happened? Is something bothering you?

MEL   Why do we live like this? Why do we pay somebody hundreds of dollars a month to live in an egg box that leaks?

EDNA   You don't look well to me, Mel. You look pale. You look haggard.

MEL   I wasn't planning to be up.
(*He rubs his stomach*)

EDNA   Why are you rubbing your stomach?

MEL   I'm not rubbing it, I'm holding it.

EDNA  Why are you holding your stomach?

MEL  It's nothing. A little indigestion. It's that crap I had for lunch.

EDNA  Where did you eat?

MEL  In a health-food restaurant. If you can't eat health food, what the hell can you eat any more?

EDNA  You're probably just hungry. Do you want me to make you something?

MEL  Nothing is safe any more. I read in the paper today two white mice at Columbia University got cancer from eating graham crackers. It was in *The New York Times.*

EDNA  Is that what's bothering you? Did you eat graham crackers today?

MEL  Food used to be so good. I used to love food. I haven't eaten food since I was thirteen years old.

EDNA  Do you want some food? I'll make you food. I remember how they made it.

MEL  I haven't had a real piece of bread in thirty years . . . If I knew what was going to happen, I would have saved some rolls when I was a kid. You can't breathe in here. *(He goes out onto the terrace)* Christ, what a stink. Fourteen stories up, you can smell the garbage from here. Why do they put garbage out in eighty-nine-degree heat? Edna, come here, I want you to smell the garbage.

EDNA  *(Comes to the door of the terrace)*  I smell it, I smell it.

MEL  You can't smell it from there. Come here where you can smell it.

EDNA  *(Walks to the edge of the terrace and inhales)*  You're right. If you really want to smell it, you have to stand right here.

MEL   This country is being buried by its own garbage. It keeps piling up higher and higher. In three years this apartment is going to be the second floor.

EDNA   What can they do, Mel? Save it up and put it out in the winter? They have to throw it out sometime. That's why they call it garbage.

MEL   I can't talk to you. I can't talk to you any more.

EDNA   Mel, I'm a human being the same as you. I get hot, I get cold, I smell garbage, I hear noise. You either live with it or you get out.
      *(Suddenly a dog howls and barks)*

MEL   If you're a human being you reserve the right to complain, to protest. When you give up that right, you don't exist any more. I protest to stinking garbage and jiggling toilets . . . and barking dogs. *(Yells out)* Shut up, goddamnit.

EDNA   Are you going to stay here and yell at the dog? Because I'm going to sleep.
      *(The dog howls again)*

MEL   How can you sleep with a dog screaming like that? *(The dog howls again.* MEL *goes to the edge of the terrace and yells down)* Keep that dog quiet. There are human beings sleeping up here. Christ Almighty!!!!

VOICE   *(From above)*   Will you be quiet. There are children up here.

MEL   *(Yelling up)*   What the hell are you yelling at me for? You looking for trouble, go down and keep the dog company.

EDNA   Mel, will you stop it! Stop it, for God's sakes!

MEL   *(Comes back in; screams at* EDNA*)*   Don't tell *me* to stop it! DON'T TELL ME TO STOP IT!

EDNA  I don't know what's gotten into you. But I'm not going to stand here and let you take it out on me . . . If it's too much for you, take a room in the public library, *but don't take it out on me.* I'm going to sleep, *good night!!*
  *(She turns angrily and heads for the bedroom. She gets almost to the bedroom door before* MEL *calls to her)*

MEL  Edna! *(She stops and turns around)* Don't go! . . . Talk to me for a few minutes, because I think I'm going out of my mind.
  *(She stops, looks at him, and comes back into the living room)*

EDNA  What is it?

MEL  I'm unraveling . . . I'm losing touch!

EDNA  You haven't been sleeping well lately.

MEL  I don't know where I am half the time. I walk down Madison Avenue, I think I'm in a foreign country.

EDNA  I know that feeling, Mel.

MEL  It's not just a feeling, something is happening to me . . . I'm losing control. I can't handle things any more. The telephone on my desk rings seven, eight times before I answer it . . . I forgot how to work the water cooler today. I stood there with an empty cup in my hand and water running all over my shoes.

EDNA  It's not just you, Mel, it's everybody. Everybody's feeling the tension these days.

MEL  Tension? If I could just feel tension, I'd give a thousand dollars to charity . . . When you're tense, you're tight, you're holding on to something. I don't know where to grab. Edna, I'm slipping, and I'm scared.

EDNA  Don't talk like that. What about seeing the analyst again?

MEL  Who? Doctor Pike? He's dead: Six years of my life, twenty-three thousand dollars. He got my money, what does he care if he gets a heart attack?

EDNA  There are other good doctors. You can see someone else.

MEL  And start all over from the beginning? "Hello. Sit down. What seems to be the trouble?" . . . It'll cost me another twenty-three thousand just to fill *this* doctor in with information I already gave the dead one.

EDNA  What about a little therapy? Maybe you just need someone to talk to for a while.

MEL  I don't know where or who I am any more. I'm disappearing, Edna. I don't need analysts, I need Lost and Found.

EDNA  Listen . . . Listen . . . What about if we get away for a couple of weeks? A two-week vacation? Someplace in the sun, away from the city. You can get two weeks' sick leave, can't you, Mel?
*(He is silent. He walks to the window and glances over at the plant)*

MEL  Even the cactus is dying. Strongest plant in the world, only has to be watered twice a year. Can't make a go of it on Eighty-eighth and Second.

EDNA  Mel, answer me. What about getting away? Can't you ask them for two weeks off?

MEL  *(Makes himself a scotch)*  Yes, I can ask them for two weeks off. What worries me is that they'll ask me to take the other fifty weeks as well.
*(He drinks)*

EDNA  You? What are you talking about? You've been there twenty-two years . . . Mel, is that it? Is that what's been bothering you? You're worried about losing your job?

MEL   I'm not worried about losing it. I'm worried about keeping it. Losing it is easy.

EDNA   Has something happened? Have they said anything?

MEL   They don't have to say anything. The company lost three million dollars this year. Suddenly they're looking to save pennies. The vice-president of my department has been using the same paper clip for three weeks now. A sixty-two-year-old man with a duplex on Park Avenue and a house in Southampton running around the office, screaming, "Where's my paper clip?"

EDNA   But they haven't actually said anything to you.

MEL   They closed the executive dining room. Nobody goes out to lunch any more. They bring sandwiches from home. Top executives, making eighty thousand dollars a year, eating egg-salad sandwiches over the wastepaper basket.

EDNA   Nothing has happened yet, Mel. There's no point in worrying about it now.

MEL   No one comes to work late any more. Everyone's afraid if you're not there on time, they'll sell your desk.

EDNA   And what if they did? We'd live, we'd get by. You'd get another job somewhere.

MEL   Where? I'm gonna be forty-seven years old in January. Forty-seven! They could get two twenty-three-and-a-half-year-old kids for half my money.

EDNA   All right, suppose something *did* happen? Suppose you *did* lose your job? It's not the end of the world. We

don't have to live in the city. We could move somewhere
in the country, or even out west.

MEL    And what do I do for a living? Become a middle-aged
cowboy? Maybe they'll put me in charge of rounding up
the elderly cattle . . . What's the matter with you?

EDNA    The girls are in college now, we have enough to
see them through. We don't need much for the two of
us.

MEL    You need a place to live, you need clothing, you
need food. A can of polluted tuna fish is still eighty-five
cents.

EDNA    We could move to Europe. To Spain. Two people
could live for fifteen hundred dollars a year in Spain.

MEL    *(Nods)    Spanish* people. I'm forty-seven years old, with
arthritis in my shoulder and high blood pressure—you
expect me to raise goats and live in a cave?

EDNA    You could work there, get some kind of a job.

MEL    An advertising account executive? In Barcelona?
They've probably been standing at the dock waiting for
years for someone like that.

EDNA    *(Angrily)*    What is it they have here that's so damned
hard to give up? *What is it you'll miss so badly, for God's
sakes?*

MEL    I'm not through with my life yet . . . I still have value,
I still have worth.

EDNA    What kind of a life is this? You live like some kind
of a caged animal in a Second Avenue zoo that's too hot
in one room, too cold in another, overcharged for a
growth on the side of the building they call a terrace that
can't support a cactus plant, let alone two human beings.

Is this what you call a worthwhile life? Banging on walls and jiggling toilets?

MEL *(Shouts)* You think it's any better in Sunny Spain? Go swimming on the beach, it'll take you the rest of the summer to scrape the oil off.

EDNA Forget Spain. There are other places to live.

MEL Maine? Vermont maybe? You think it's all rolling hills and maple syrup? They have more people on welfare up there than they have pancakes. Washington? Oregon? Unemployed lumberjacks are sitting around sawing legs off chairs; they have nothing else to do.

EDNA I will go anywhere in the world you want to go, Mel. I will live in a cave, a hut or a tree. I will live on a raft in the Amazon jungle if that's what you want to do.

MEL All right, call a travel agency. Get two economy seats to Bolivia. We'll go to Abercrombie's tomorrow, get a couple of pith helmets and a spear gun.

EDNA Don't talk to me like I'm insane.

MEL I'm halfway there, you might as well catch up.

EDNA I am trying to offer reasonable suggestions. I am not responsible. I am not the one who's doing this to you.

MEL I didn't say you were, Edna.

EDNA Then what do you want from me? *What do you want from anyone?*

MEL *(Buries his face in his hands)* Just a little breathing space . . . just for a little while. *(The phone rings.* MEL *looks up at* EDNA*)* Who could that be? *(*EDNA *shakes her head, not knowing)* It couldn't be the office, could it?

EDNA At a quarter to three in the morning?

MEL   Maybe they got the night watchman to fire me, they'll save a day's salary.
    *(It keeps ringing)*

EDNA   Answer it, Mel, I'm nervous.
    (MEL *picks up the phone*)

MEL *(Into the phone)*   Hello? . . . Yes? . . . Yes, Apartment 14A, what about it? . . . *What??? I'm keeping YOU up???* Who the hell do you think got *me* up to get *you* up in the first place? . . . Don't tell me you got a plane leaving for Stuttgart in the morning . . . I'll talk as loud as I damn well please. This isn't a sublet apartment, I'm a regular American tenant . . . Go ahead and bang on the wall. You'll get a bang right back on yours. *(He covers the phone, then says to* EDNA*)* If she bangs, I want you to bang back.

EDNA   Mel, what are you starting in for?
    *(From the other side of the wall, we hear a loud banging)*

MEL   Okay, bang back.

EDNA   Mel, it's a quarter to three. Leave them alone, they'll go to sleep.

MEL   Will you bang back?!

EDNA   If I bang back, she's just going to bang back at me.

MEL   Will you bang back!!!?

EDNA   I'll bang, I'll bang!
    *(She bangs twice on the wall)*

MEL *(Into the phone)*   All right? *(From the other side of the wall, they bang again.* MEL *says to* EDNA*)* Bang back! *(She bangs again. They bang from the other side again. He repeats his instructions to* EDNA*)* Bang back! *(She bangs again. They bang again)* Bang back!
    *(She bangs. The stage goes black, then the curtain falls.*

*The house remains in darkness. A screen drops and the News Logo appears. We hear Roger Keating with the Six O'Clock Report)*

VOICE OF ROGER KEATING *(In the darkness)* This is Roger Keating and the *Six O'Clock Report* . . . New York was hit with its third strike of the week. This time the city employees of thirty-seven New York hospitals walked out at 3 P.M. this afternoon. The Mayor's office has been flooded with calls, as hundred of patients and elderly sick people have complained of lack of food, clean sheets and medicines. One seventy-nine-year-old patient in Lenox Hill Hospital fell in the corridor, broke his leg and was treated by a seventy-three-year-old patient who had just recovered from a gall-bladder operation . . . Two of the most cold-blooded robbers in the city's history today made off with four thousand dollars, stolen from the New York City Home for the Blind. Police believe it may have been the same men who got away with thirty-six hundred dollars on Tuesday from the New York Cat and Dog Hospital . . . Water may be shut off tomorrow, says the New York Commissioner of Health, because of an anonymous phone call made to the bureau this morning, threatening to dump fifty pounds of chemical pollutants in the city's reservoirs. The unidentified caller, after making his threat, concluded with, "It's gonna be dry tomorrow, baby." . . . And from the office of Police Commissioner Murphy, a report that the number of apartment house burglaries has risen seven point two percent in August.

*It is afternoon, a few days later.*

*At the curtain's rise, the room is in a shambles. Chairs are overturned; drawers are pulled open, their contents scattered all over the floor; the bookcase has been cleared of half of its shelves and articles of clothing are strewn about the room. It is obvious what has happened.*

EDNA *is on the phone. She is shaking.*

EDNA *(Sobbing)* Edison, Mrs. Edna Edison . . . I've just been robbed . . . I just walked in, they took everything . . . Edison . . . I just walked in, I found the door open, they must have just left . . . 385 East 88th Street . . . Two minutes sooner, I could have been killed . . . Apartment 14A . . . I don't know yet. Television, the record player, books, clothing . . . They took lots of clothing. My dresses, my coats, all my husband's suits—there's not a thing left in his closet . . . I haven't checked the drawers yet . . . Would you, please? Send somebody right away . . . I'm all alone. My husband isn't home from work yet . . . *Mrs. Edna Edison.* I could have been killed. Thank you. *(She hangs up, then turns and looks at the room. She crosses the room, lifts a chair up and sets it right. Then she goes over to the bureau and starts to look through the drawers. As she discovers new things are missing, she sobs louder)* All right . . . Calm down . . . A drink, I have to have a drink *(She rushes into the kitchen, gets a glass and a few cubes of ice from the refrigerator, then rushes back out into the living room. She rushes to the bar and looks. There are no bottles)* The liquor's gone. They took the liquor. *(She puts the glass down, slumps into a chair, and sobs.)* Valium . . . I want a Valium. *(She gets up and rushes down the small corridor, disappearing into the bedroom. We hear noises as she must be looking through ransacked medicine chests. There are a few moments of silence.* EDNA *has probably fallen onto the bed, sobbing, for all we know. The front door is unlocked and* MEL *enters. He carries his suit jacket and the New York* Post. *His shirt sleeves are rolled up and he looks hot. He closes the door and hangs his jacket in the closet. Consumed with his own thoughts, he doesn't seem to even notice the room. He moves over to the chair, falls into it exhausted, puts his head back and sighs . . . His eyes open, then he looks at the room for almost the first time. He looks around the room, bewildered. From the bedroom we hear* EDNA's *voice)* Mel? . . . Is that you, Mel?

> (MEL *is still looking at the room, puzzled.* EDNA *appears cautiously from the bedroom. She comes in, holding a vase by the thin end, and looks at* MEL)

MEL   Didn't Mildred come in to clean today?

EDNA   *(Puts the vase down)*   Not today . . . Mondays and Thursdays.

MEL   What happened here? . . . Why is this place such a mess?

EDNA   We've been robbed.
> (MEL *looks at her in a state of shock . . . He slowly rises and then looks at the room in a new perspective)*

MEL   What do you mean, robbed?

EDNA   *(Starts to cry)*   Robbed! Robbed! What does robbed mean? They come in, they take things out! *They robbed us!!!*

MEL   *(He keeps turning, looking at the room in disbelief—not knowing where to look first)*   I don't understand . . . What do you mean, someone just walked in and robbed us?

EDNA   What do you think? . . . They called up and made an appointment? *We've been robbed!*

MEL  All right, calm down. Take it easy, Edna. I'm just asking a simple question. What happened? What did they get?

EDNA  I don't know yet. I was out shopping. I was gone five minutes. I came back, I found it like this.

MEL  You couldn't have been gone five minutes. Look at this place.

EDNA  *Five minutes*, that's all I was gone.

MEL  Five minutes, heh? Then we'd better call the FBI, because every crook in New York must have been in here.

EDNA  Then that's who was here, because I was only gone five minutes.

MEL  When you came back into the building did you notice anyone suspicious-looking?

EDNA  *Everyone* in this building is suspicious-looking.

MEL  You didn't see anybody carrying any bundles or packages?

EDNA  I didn't notice.

MEL  What do you mean, you didn't notice?

EDNA  I didn't notice. You think I look for people leaving the building with my television set?

MEL  They took the television? *(He starts for the bedroom, then stops)* A *brand new* color television?

EDNA  They're not looking for 1948 Philcos. It was here. They took it. I can't get a breath out.

MEL  All right, sit there. I'll get a drink.

EDNA  *(Sitting down)* I don't want a drink.

MEL  A little scotch. It'll calm you down.

EDNA  It won't calm me down, because there's no scotch. They took the scotch too.

MEL  *All* the scotch?

EDNA  All the scotch.

MEL  The Chivas Regal too?

EDNA  No, they're going to take the cheap scotch and leave the Chivas Regal. They took it all, they cleaned us out.

MEL  (*Gnashing his teeth*) Sons of bitches. (*He runs to the terrace door, opens it, steps out on the terrace and yells out*) Sons of bitches! (*He closes the door and comes back in*) All in five minutes, eh? They must have been gorillas to lift all that in five minutes.

EDNA  Leave me alone.

MEL  (*Gnashing his teeth again*) Sons of bitches.

EDNA  Stop swearing, the police will be here any minute. I just called them.

MEL  You called the police?

EDNA  Didn't I just say that?

MEL  Did you tell them we were robbed?

EDNA  Why else would I call them? I'm not friendly with the police. What kind of questions are you asking me? What's wrong with you?

MEL  All right, calm down, because you're hysterical.

EDNA  I am not hysterical.

MEL  You're hysterical.

EDNA  You're *making* me hysterical. Don't you understand? My house has just been robbed.

MEL   What am I, a boarder? My house has been robbed too. My color television and my Chivas Regal is missing the same as yours.

EDNA   You didn't walk in and find it. *I* did.

MEL   What's the difference who found it? There's still nothing to drink and nothing to watch.
EDNA   Don't yell at me. I'm just as upset as you are.

MEL   I'm sorry. I'm excited, too. I don't mean to yell at you. *(Starts for the bedroom)* Let me get you a Valium, it'll calm you down.

EDNA   I don't want a Valium.

MEL   Take one. You'll feel better.

EDNA   I'm not taking a Valium.

MEL   Why are you so stubborn?

EDNA   I'm not stubborn. We don't have any. They took the Valiums.

MEL   *(Stops)*   They took the Valiums?

EDNA   The whole medicine chest. Valiums, Seconals, aspirin, shaving cream, toothpaste, razor blades. They left your toothbrush. You want to go in and brush your teeth, you can still do it.

MEL   *(Smiles, disbelieving)*   I don't believe you. *I don't believe you!*
      *(*MEL *looks at her, then storms off and disappears into the bedroom.* EDNA *gets up and picks up a book from the floor. From the far recesses of the bathroom we hear* MEL *scream:)*

MEL   *(Offstage)*   DIRTY BASTARDS!!! *(*EDNA *is holding the book upside down and shaking it, hoping some concealed item will fall out. It doesn't.* MEL *storms back into living*

23

*room)* I hope they die. I hope the car they stole to get away in hits a tree and turns over and burns up and they all die!

EDNA You read about it every day. And when it happens to you, you can't believe it.

MEL A television I can understand. Liquor I can understand. But shaving cream? Hair spray? How much are they going to get for a roll of dental floss?

EDNA They must have been desperate. They took everything they could carry. *(Shakes the book one last time)* They even found my kitchen money.

MEL What kitchen money?

EDNA I kept my kitchen money in here. Eighty-five dollars.

MEL In cash? Why do you keep cash in a book?

EDNA So no one will find it! Where else am I gonna keep it?

MEL In a jar. In the sugar. Some place they're not going to look.

EDNA They looked in the medicine chest, you think they're not going to look in the sugar?

MEL *Nobody looks in sugar!*

EDNA Nobody steals dental floss and mouthwash. Only sick people. Only that's who live in the world today. *Sick, sick, sick people!*
(*She sits, emotionally wrung out.* MEL *comes over to her and puts his arm on her shoulder, comforting her)*

MEL It's all right . . . It's all right, Edna . . . As long as you weren't hurt, that's the important thing.
(*He looks through the papers on the table)*

EDNA Can you imagine if I had walked in and found them here? What would I have done, Mel?

MEL   You were very lucky, Edna. Very lucky.

EDNA   But what would I have done?

MEL   What's the difference? You didn't walk in and find them.

EDNA   But supposing I did? What would I have done?

MEL   You'd say, "Excuse me," close the door and come back later. What would you do, sit and watch? Why do you ask me such questions? It didn't happen, did it?

EDNA   It *almost* happened. If I walked in here five minutes sooner.

MEL   (*Walking away from her*) You couldn't have been gone only five minutes . . . It took the Seven Santini Brothers two days to move everything in, three junkies aren't gonna move it all out in five minutes.

EDNA   Seven minutes, eight minutes, what's the difference?

MEL   (*Opens the door, looks at the lock*) The lock isn't broken, it's not jimmied. I don't even know how they got in here.

EDNA   Maybe they found my key in the street.

MEL   (*Closes the door. Looks at her*) What do you mean, "found your key"? Don't you have your key?

EDNA   No, I lost it. I thought it was somewhere in the house, but maybe I lost it in the street.

MEL   If you didn't have your key, how were you going to get back in the house when you went shopping?

EDNA   I left the door open.

MEL   You—left—the—door—open???

EDNA   I didn't have a key, how was I going to get back in the house?

MEL *So you left the door open?* In a city with the highest crime rate in the history of the world, *you left the door open?*

EDNA What was I doing to do? Take the furniture with me? I was only gone five minutes. How did they know I was going to leave the door open?

MEL They know! They know! A door opens, it doesn't lock, the whole junkie world lights up. "Door open, fourteenth floor, Eighty-eighth Street and Second Avenue." They know!

EDNA They don't know anything. They have to go around trying doors.

MEL And what did you think? They were going to try every door in this house except yours? "Let's leave 14A alone, fellas, it looks like a nice door."

EDNA If they're going to go around trying doors, they have twenty-three hours and fifty-five minutes a day to try them. I didn't think they would try ours the five minutes I was out of the house. I gambled! I lost!

MEL What kind of gamble is that to take? If you lose, they get everything. If you win, they rob somebody else.

EDNA I *had* to shop. There was nothing in the house to eat tonight.

MEL All right, now you have something to eat and nothing to eat it with . . . Why didn't you call up and have them send it?

EDNA Because I shop in a cheap store that doesn't deliver. I am trying to save us money because you got me so worried the other night. I was just trying to save us money . . . Look how much money I saved us.
(EDNA *starts to pick up things*)

MEL   What are you doing?

EDNA   We can't leave everything like this. I want to clean up.

MEL   Now?

EDNA   The place is a mess. We have people coming over in a few minutes.

MEL   The *police?* You want the place to look nice for the police? . . . You're worried they're going to put it down in their books, "bad housekeeper"? . . . Leave it alone. Maybe they'll find some clues.

EDNA   I can't find out what's missing until I put everything back in its place.

MEL   What do you mean? You know what's missing. The television, the liquor, the kitchen money, the medicine chest and the hi-fi . . . That's it, isn't it? *(Pause)* Isn't it? *(EDNA looks away)* Okay, what else did they get?

EDNA   Am I a detective? Look, you'll find out.
*(He glares at her and looks around the room, not know-ing where to begin. He decides to check the bedroom. He storms down the hall and disappears.* EDNA, *knowing what to soon expect, sits on a chair in the dining area and stares out the window. She takes out a hanky and wipes some dirt from the window sill.* MEL *returns calmly—at least outwardly calm. He takes a deep breath)*

MEL   Where are my suits?

EDNA   They were there this morning. They're not there now. They must have taken your suits.

MEL   *(Still trying to be calm)*   Seven suits? Three sports jack-ets? Eight pairs of slacks?

EDNA   If that's what you had, that's what they got.

MEL   I'm lucky my tuxedo is in the cleaners.

EDNA   *(Still staring out the window)*   They sent it back this morning.

MEL   Well, they did a good job of it . . . Cleaned me out . . . Left a pair of khaki pants and my golf hat . . . Anybody asks us out to dinner this week, ask them if it's all right if I wear khaki pants and a golf hat. DIRTY BASTARDS!!!!
  *(In what can only be described as an insane tantrum, he picks up some ashtrays from the sideboard and throws them to the floor of the kitchen, continuing uncontrollably until all his energy and his vitriol have been exhausted . . . He stands there panting)*

EDNA   It's just things, Mel. Just some old suits and coats. We can replace them. We'll buy new ones. Can't we, Mel?

MEL   With what? . . . *With what?* They *fired* me.
  *(He sits, his back to the wall)*

EDNA   Oh, my God. Don't tell me.

MEL   Well, I'm telling you. *They fired me!* . . . Me, Hal Chesterman, Mike Ambrozi, Dave Polichek, Arnold Strauss . . . Two others, I can't even remember their names . . . Seven of us, in one fell swoop. *Fired!*

EDNA   *(She is so distraught that she can't even stir in her chair)* Oh, Mel, I'm so sorry . . .

MEL   They called us into the office one at a time. They didn't even have to say it, we knew. We saw it coming. Even the secretaries knew. They couldn't look at you when you said good morning . . . Eighty-five-dollar-a-week girls were bringing me coffee and Danish and not charging me for it. I knew right away.

EDNA   Oh, Mel, Mel, Mel . . .

MEL   They said they had no choice. They had to make cuts right down the line . . . Seven executives, twelve sales-men, twenty-four in office help—forty-three people in one afternoon . . . It took three elevators two trips to get rid of all the losers . . . Wait'll the coffee and Danish man comes in tomorrow, he'll throw himself out the window.

EDNA   And then you come home to this. To get fired and then to come home and find your house has been robbed.

MEL   It didn't happen today. It happened Monday.

EDNA   Monday? You mean you've known for four days and you haven't said a word to me?

MEL   I didn't know how to tell you, I couldn't work up the courage. I thought maybe another job would turn up, a miracle would happen . . . Miracles don't happen when you're forty-seven . . . When Moses saw the burning bush, he must have been twenty-three, twenty-four, the most. Never forty-seven.
   *(He goes into the kitchen, gets a can of beer)*

EDNA   What have you done since Monday? Where have you been? What did you do all day?

MEL   *(Comes out of the kitchen, sits down, and drinks)*   In the mornings I made phone calls, tried to see a few people. When you're looking for help, you'd be surprised how many people are out to lunch at ten-thirty in the morning . . . In the afternoons? *(He shrugs)* I went to museums, an auction, the office-furniture show at the Coliseum . . . I saw an Italian movie, I saw a Polish movie . . . I saw two dirty movies . . . I met Dave Polichek at the dirty movie. We both lied. Said we were killing time until our next appointment. Some important appointments. I went to Cen-tral Park and he went to the Ripley Wax Museum.

EDNA   You should have come home, Mel.

MEL   Why? I had a very nice bench in the park near the Wollman Skating Rink. For lunch I had my jelly apple and my Fanta orange drink.

EDNA   Oh, Mel, I can't bear it.

MEL   I came very close to having an affair with a seventy-three-year-old English nanny. We hit it off very well but the baby didn't like me. *(At this point* EDNA *gets up and quickly rushes to* MEL, *who is still sitting. He reaches up and grabs her around the waist, holding on for dear life)* I'll be all right, Edna. I don't want you to worry about me. I'll be all right.

EDNA   I know you will, Mel. I know it.

MEL   I'll find another job, you'll see.

EDNA   Of course you will.

MEL   You'll take down the living room drapes, make me a suit, and I'll look for another job.

EDNA *(Hugs him)*   Oh Mel, we'll be all right. We will.
      *(They break)*

MEL   I played two innings of softball yesterday.

EDNA   You didn't.
      *(He sits on the sofa; she resumes picking up items)*

MEL *(Nods)*   Mm-hmm. With a day camp for fourteen-year-olds . . . Harvey, the right fielder, had to go for a violin lesson, so I played the last two innings.

EDNA   And you hit a home run?

MEL   I struck out, dropped two fly balls and lost the game . . . They wanted to kill me.

EDNA   I wish I'd been there.

MEL   I know I can make the team, I just have to get my timing back. If I don't find a job maybe I'll go back to camp this summer.

EDNA   It would take me two minutes to sew in your name tapes. You want to think about it while I make you a cup of coffee?
   *(She starts for the kitchen)*

MEL   They didn't get the coffee? They left us the coffee? How come?

EDNA   Robbers never go into the kitchen.

MEL   Then why didn't you leave the money in the sugar jar?

EDNA   Mel, we're insured. We'll get all the money back.

MEL   We're lucky if we get half. You think you get two hundred dollars for a two-hundred-dollar coat? They depreciate. You put it on once, button it, it's worth forty dollars.

EDNA   Then we'll get half the money back.

MEL   Then the premiums go up. You get robbed once and it costs you twice as much to protect half of what you used to have.

EDNA   *(Comes out of the kitchen)* Mel, please don't worry about the money. We have something put aside. We're not extravagant. We can live comfortably for a while.

MEL   With two girls in college? With our rent, with our food bills, with nothing coming it? . . . We have to get out, Edna. We have to get out of everything.
   *(He paces around the room)*

EDNA   I'll go wherever you want, Mel.

MEL    I don't mean out of here. Out of obligations. Out of things we don't need that are choking us. I'm gonna quit the gym. I don't need a gym for two hundred and fifty dollars a year. I'll run around the bedroom, it's the only way to keep warm in there anyway . . . And we don't need the Museum of Modern Art. We can watch *Duck Soup* on television. *(Picks up some magazines)* And these goddamn magazines. I don't want *Time, Life* or *Newsweek* any more, you understand. I'm not going to spend my last few dollars to find out that unemployment went up this year.

   *(He throws them into the wastebasket)*

EDNA    We don't need *any* of them. We never did, Mel.

MEL    *(Looking around, throwing some more junk into the basket)* The garbage! The garbage that we buy every year. Useless, meaningless garbage that fills up the house until you throw it out there and it becomes garbage again and *stinks* up the house. For what? For *what*, Edna?

EDNA    I don't know, Mel.

MEL    Two dollars' worth of food that comes in three dollars' worth of wrapping. Telephone calls to find out what time it is because you're too lazy to look at a clock . . . The food we never ate, the books we never read, the records we never played. *(He picks up a little thing off the bar)* Look at this! Eight and a half dollars for a musical whiskey pourer. *Eight and a half dollars!* God forbid we should get a little bored while we're pouring our whiskey! Toys! Toys, novelties, gimmicks, trivia, garbage, crap, HORSESHIT!!!

   *(He hurls the basket to the floor)*

EDNA    No more. We'll never buy another thing, Mel. I promise. I promise.

MEL *(He is seething with anger)* Twenty-two years I gave them. What did I give them twenty-two years of my life for? A musical whiskey pourer? It's my *life* that's been poured down the drain. Where's the music? Where's a cute little tune? They kick you out after twenty-two years, they ought to have a goddamned brass band.

EDNA All right, don't get upset. You're going to get yourself sick.

MEL You know where my music is? *(He goes over to the wall and points)* There! There it is! It's playing on the other side of that wall. *(Screaming) There's my music after twenty-two years.* *(He grabs his chest, grimacing)* Ohh!

EDNA What is it, Mel? What's the matter?

MEL I got pains in my chest. It's nothing, don't worry. It's not a heart attack.

EDNA *(Nervously)* What do you mean? Why do you say it's not a heart attack?

MEL Because it's not a heart attack. It's pains in my chest.

EDNA Why are you having pains in your chest?

MEL BECAUSE I DON'T HAVE A JOB. BECAUSE I DON'T HAVE A SUIT TO WEAR! BECAUSE I'M HAVING A GODDAMNED BREAKDOWN AND THEY DIDN'T EVEN LEAVE ME WITH A PILL TO TAKE! *(He rushes out onto the terrace again and screams)* BASTARDS! . . . YOU DIRTY BASTARDS!
*(Suddenly a* VOICE, *probably from the terrace above, yells down)*

VOICE Shut up, down there! There are children up here!

MEL *(Leans over the terrace wall and yells up)* Don't you yell at me! They took everything! EVERYTHING!

33

They left me with a goddamned pair of pants *and a golf hat!*

VOICE   There are children up here! Are you drunk or something?

MEL   Drunk? Drunk on what? They got my liquor . . . You wanna keep your children, lock 'em up. Don't you tell me you got children up there.

EDNA   Mel, please. You're going to get yourself sick.

VOICE   Don't you have any respect for anyone else?

MEL   *(Screaming up)*   Respect? I got respect for my ass, that's what I got respect for! That's all anybody respects . . .
    *(And suddenly MEL gets hit with a torrent of water, obviously from a large bucket. He is drenched, soaked through—completely, devastatingly and humiliatingly . . . He comes back into the room. He is too stunned and shocked to be able to say a word)*

EDNA   Oh, God. Oh, God, Mel.

MEL   *(Very calmly and quietly, almost like a child who has been hurt)*   That's a terrible thing to do . . . That's a mean, terrible thing to do.
    *(And he sits down on a chair and begins to sob. He just quietly sits there and sobs . . . EDNA runs out to the terrace and yells up)*

EDNA   God will punish you for that . . . I apologize for my husband's language, but God will punish you for that. *(She is crying too. She runs back to MEL, picks up some linens from the floor, and begins to dry his face and his head)* It's all right, Mel. It's all right, baby . . .

MEL   That's a terrible thing to do to a person . . . I would never do that to anyone.

EDNA *(Wiping him)* Never. You're too good, Mel, too decent. You would never do that . . . It's going to be all right, Mel, I promise. You'll get another job, you'll see . . . And we'll move away from here. Someplace far away . . . You know what we could do? You're so good with kids, you love being with them, we could start a summer camp . . . You would be the head of the camp and I would do the cooking and the girls can be the riding instructors and the swimming instructors. You would like that, wouldn't you, Mel? We'll just have to save some money, that's all. And if you don't get another job right away, I can always be a secretary again. I can work, I'm strong, Mel . . . But you mustn't get sick. You mustn't get sick and die because I don't want to live in this world without you . . . I don't like it here! . . . I don't want you to leave me alone here . . . We'll show them, Mel. We'll show them all.

*(She continues to wipe his ears as the curtain slowly falls)*

# ACT TWO

*It is about six weeks later. It is mid-September, about one in the afternoon.*

*A radio is on, playing music.*

*From the bedroom we hear dull, rhythmic thumping sounds. The thump is repeated every few seconds.* MEL *emerges from the bedroom. He is wearing khaki slacks, a pajama top, a bathrobe with the belt half open, and a pair of slippers. He has a baseball glove on his left hand and a baseball in his right. He keeps throwing the ball into the glove . . . thump . . . thump . . . thump . . .*

*Six weeks of unemployment have turned* MEL *into a different man. His eyes seem to be sunken into his sockets; he has rings under his eyes and seems to shave only sporadically. There is also a grimness about him, an anger, an hostility, the look of a man who is suffering from a deep depression coupled with a tendency to paranoia.*

*He comes into the living room aimlessly. He has no place to go and no desire to go there. He wanders around the room not seeming to see anything. He walks in all the available walking spaces in the living room and dining room, like a prisoner taking his daily exercise. He keeps banging the ball into his glove with increasing intensity . . . thump . . . thump . . . thump . . .*

*He throws the ball up against the wall where the banging came from, then he crosses into the kitchen looking for something to eat.*

*Someone puts a key in the door; it opens.* EDNA *rushes in, dressed smartly in a suit and carrying a small bundle of food in a brown paper bag. She throws down a magazine, calls out:*

EDNA  Mel? . . . Mel, I'm home. (*She closes the door and enters the living room, turns off the radio, and then goes into the kitchen)* You must be starved. I'll have your lunch in a second. *(She takes things out of the package)* I couldn't get out of the office until a quarter to one and then I had to wait fifteen minutes for a bus . . . God, the traffic on Third Avenue during lunch hour . . . I got a cheese soufflé in Schrafft's, is that all right? I just don't have time to fix anything today, Mr. Cooperman wants me back before two o'clock, we're suddenly swamped with work this week . . . He asked if I would come in on Saturdays from now until Christmas but I told him I didn't think I could. *(She goes into the kitchen and gets out some pots)* I mean we could use the extra money but I don't think I want to spend Saturdays in that office too. We see each other little enough now as it is . . . Come in and talk to me while I'm cooking, Mel, I've only got about thirty-five minutes today. *(EDNA has put the casserole on the table and is now going into the kitchen, setting up two places with dishes and silverware)* My feet are absolutely killing me. I don't know why they gave me a desk because I haven't had a chance to sit at it in a month . . . Hi, love. I bought you *Sports Illustrated* . . . Mr. Cooperman told me there's a terrific story in there about the Knicks, he thought you might be interested in it. *(MEL tosses the magazine aside with some contempt)* You just can't move up Third Avenue because there's one of those protest parades up Fifth Avenue, or down Fifth Avenue, whichever way they protest . . . Fifteen thousand women screaming, "Save the environment," and they're all wearing leopard coats . . . God, the hypocrisy . . . Come on, sit down, I've got some tomato juice first. *(She pours tomato juice into two glasses. MEL listlessly moves over to the table and sits down)* Isn't that terrible about the Commissioner of Police? I mean *kidnapping* the New York Commissioner of Police? Isn't that insane? I mean if the cops can't find him, they can't find anybody. *(She sits down, picks up her glass of juice and takes a sip)* Oh, God, that's good. That's the first food I've had since eight o'clock this morning. We're so busy there we don't even have time for a coffee break . . . He's going to ask me to work nights, I know it, and I just don't know what to say to him . . . I mean he's been so nice to me, he buys me sandwiches two or three times a week, not that I don't deserve it, the way I've been working this past month, but I just don't want to spend any nights down there because I don't even have the strength to talk when I get home any more . . . I don't know where I'm getting the energy, I must have been saving it up for the past twenty-two years. *(She sips again)* I've got to stop talking because I'm all wound up and I'll never stop . . . How are you, darling? You feeling all right? (MEL *sits, staring into his tomato juice)* Mel? You all right?

MEL *(Mumbles something affirmative)* Mmm.

EDNA *(Looks at him)* Don't feel like talking much?

MEL  Mmm.

EDNA  Oh, come on, Mel. I've got to leave in about thirty minutes and I probably won't get home until seven o'clock. Talk to me . . . What did you do today?

MEL *(He looks at her. He waits a long time before he answers)* I took a walk.

EDNA  Oh, that's nice. Where?

MEL  From the bedroom to the living room . . .

EDNA *(Nervous about his frame of mind, but restrains herself to keep from putting him on edge)* Is that all?

MEL  No. I walked back into the bedroom . . . Once I went into the kitchen for a glass of water. What else you want to know?

EDNA  Nothing. You don't feel like talking, that's all right.

MEL   I feel like talking. You want to hear about the rest of my morning?

EDNA *(Sensing his anxiety)*   I said it's all right, Mel.

MEL   I looked out the window three times, listened to Martha Deane and went to the toilet, which is still flushing. I didn't jiggle it, I know you like to do it when you get home.

EDNA *(Sighs, puts down her glass)*   All right, what's the matter, Mel?

MEL   Nothing. I'm telling you about my terrific morning. You ready for some really exciting news? Martha Deane's guest tomorrow is the Galloping Gourmet. Isn't that exciting? He's going to give the secret recipes of five famous celebrities and we're going to have to guess whose casserole is whose . . . Too bad you're going to miss it.

EDNA   You didn't sleep well again last night, did you?

MEL   Last night? Was last night the night before this morning? I get them mixed up. I'm so busy with my life.

EDNA   I thought you were going to take a walk in the park this morning.

MEL   There is no place left for me to walk. I have walked on every path, every bridge and every stone. I know every squirrel in the park and I know where they all hide their nuts.

EDNA   I know how cooped up you feel when you stay in the house all day. Maybe we can have lunch in the zoo tomorrow?

MEL   I am *not* going to the zoo. I've been there every day for a month. When I walk by, the monkeys nudge each other and say, "He's here again."

EDNA   I just thought you might get some exercise. Get into a softball game or something.

MEL   There are no softball games. It's September, my whole team is in school.

EDNA   They get out at three o'clock. You could wait for them.

MEL   *(His voice rising)* I'm seven years older than the father of the pitcher. I am not going to wait for kids to get out of school so I can have someone to play with.

EDNA   *(Controlling herself)* There is no reason to scream at me, Mel.

MEL   I'm sorry. I'm alone a lot, I forgot what the normal voice range is. Is this any better?

EDNA   Never mind, Mel . . . Did anybody call?

MEL   Your mother. We exchanged recipes.

EDNA   *(She drums her fingers on the table, trying to control herself)* Anyone else?

MEL   I am not an answering service. You want me to answer phones, hire me. I need the work.

EDNA   I take it then there was nothing in the paper today.

MEL   About what?

EDNA   You know about what, Mel. About a job.

MEL   Yes. Mount Sinai Hospital is looking for surgical technicians. The problem is my slacks are khaki and they require white.

EDNA   I was just asking, Mel.

MEL   And I'm just answering. There's a Puerto Rican luncheonette in East Harlem that's looking for a bilin-

gual counterman. And Delta Airlines is looking for hostesses, but I don't want to be away from home that much.
Don't you agree?

EDNA   Mel, please stop it.

MEL   You know what I think my best bet is? Maurice Le
Peu in Queens is looking for a hair stylist. I thought I'd
practice on you tonight, and if you didn't go bald, I'd give
him a call tomorrow.

EDNA   *(Throws her napkin down angrily)*   What's wrong with
you? *What's wrong with you today?*

MEL   *(Slams his napkin down violently)*   Today? Today? . . .
How about seven weeks? How about almost two months
walking around this apartment like a goddamned prisoner?
I used to walk from room to room. Now I walk along
the edges of the room so I can have longer walks . . .
I have read every page of every book in this apartment.
I have read every label of every can of food in the kitchen.
Tomorrow I'm going to read underwear sizes. After that,
I'm through. I have nothing left to live for.

EDNA   *(Gets up)*   I'm sorry, Mel. I know you're bored, I
know you're unhappy. Tell me what I can do to help you.

MEL   I'm forty-seven years old. Do you have to come home
to make me lunches?

EDNA   I *want* to make you lunches. I'm working, I have a
job, I never see you. At least this way we get to spend an
hour every day together.

MEL   Don't you see how humiliating it is? Everyone in the
building knows you come home to make me lunches. The
only ones here who get lunches cooked for them every
day are me and the six-year-old girl on the fourth floor.

EDNA   I don't care what people in this building think.

MEL   *I* care! *I CARE!!* . . . They probably think you make me take a nap too . . . I can make my own lunches. I can go out to eat.

EDNA   I was just trying to save us money.

MEL   What are you going to do in the winter when it snows, come home to put on my galoshes?

EDNA   Is this what you do all morning? Walk around the edges of the apartment thinking of things like that? Torturing yourself?

MEL   I don't have to torture *myself.* I got dogs, flushing toilets and the Red Baron's two sisters in there.

EDNA   All right, what did they do today, Mel? Tell me.

MEL   No, listen, I don't want to bother you. I know you've got your own problems at the office. You've got a living to make, don't worry about the house. That's my concern.

EDNA   I thought we agreed about my working. I thought we agreed it was all right for me to take this job until something came through for you.

MEL   I'm not complaining. You've been very nice to me. You pay the rent, buy the food, bought me a nice new sport jacket . . . Maybe next year you'll take me to Hawaii on United Airlines.

EDNA   Do you want me to quit, Mel? Do you want me to leave the job? I'll leave the minute you say so, you know I will.

MEL   Not this week. Margaret Truman has Bess Myerson on this Friday, I don't want to miss it. (EDNA *gets up and*

45

*storms into the kitchen. She stands there over the stove and bangs her fist on it in desperation. Finally, after a long silence)* You think I haven't been looking? You think I haven't tried? That's what you think, isn't it?

EDNA *(From the kitchen)* I don't, Mel. I swear I don't. I know how hard you've tried.

MEL There are *no jobs* for forty-seven-years-old men . . . *Nothing! (Picks up* The New York Times) Here! Read it! It's all in *The New York Times.* I went out in the hall and stole it from the people next door . . . *I steal newspapers, Edna!*

EDNA *(Bringing in a pot of hot food from the kitchen)* Please, let's not talk about it any more.

MEL You want milk? I can get two quarts of milk every morning. If I wear my slippers they don't hear a thing.

EDNA Stop it, Mel, I don't think that's funny.

MEL I'm just trying to contribute, Edna . . . Just trying to do my share.

EDNA *(Puts some food onto the plate)* Please eat your lunch. It's the last time. I promise I won't make it any more.

MEL Why should you? When you can be in some nice Japanese restaurant eating sukiyaki with Mr. Cooperman sitting around with your shoes off.

EDNA I have never had sukiyaki with Mr. Cooperman.

MEL How about Fettucini with Mr. Feidelson? Look, I know what goes on in offices. I used to be one of the boys too.

EDNA Well, I am not "one of the girls."

MEL How come you get home at seven o'clock when everyone knows nobody works past five o'clock any more.

EDNA    *I* work past five o'clock.

MEL    Where? At Charley O's? Listen, I understand. A little drink to unwind before you go home to face the little man.

EDNA    I don't believe what I'm hearing.

MEL    You used to believe it when *I* came home at seven o'clock . . . You think it's a picnic sitting home all day wondering what's going on in that office? Try it sometime.

EDNA    I feel like I'm watching my whole life running backwards on a movie screen.

MEL    Maybe that's why I can't get a job. Maybe if I put on a wig, some high heels and a pair of hot pants, they'd hire me in a second.

EDNA    *(Puts down the dish)* I'll leave the soufflé here. Eat it or not, do whatever you want. I'm leaving. I can't talk to you when you're like this.

MEL    *(Mocking)* Have a good day, darling. Don't work too hard. Leave me some quarters for the laundromat.

EDNA    *(Starts for the door, then stops)* You know what I would suggest, Mel?

MEL    What? What would you suggest, Edna?

EDNA    I suggest you either get a very tight grip on yourself . . . or you look for someone to help you.

MEL    I don't need any help . . . I'm retired. I got it made.

EDNA    You know what I'm talking about. Medical help. A doctor. Some doctor who can talk to you and straighten you out because I am *running out of energy and patience!*

MEL    *(Looks at her and smiles)* You think it's all in my mind, don't you? . . . My God, you don't have the slightest

47

inkling of what's been going on. You are so naïve, it's ridiculous.

EDNA  What are you talking about, Mel? What's been going on?

MEL  *(Smirking, as though he has some secret)*  You think it's just by accident I can't find any work? You think it's just the breaks? I'm having a bad streak of luck, is that what you think?

EDNA  I think it's the times, Mel. We are going through bad times.

MEL  You have no suspicion of the truth, do you? None at all?

EDNA  What truth? What truth are you talking about, Mel?

MEL  I'm talking about the *plot*, Edna. The *plot*.
*(She looks at him for a long time)*

EDNA  What plot, Mel?

MEL  *(He stares at her incredulously, then laughs)*  "What plot, Mel?" . . . I'm telling you about the plot and all you can say is, "What plot, Mel?"

EDNA  I don't know what plot you're talking about. You mentioned there's a plot and all I can think of to say is, "What plot, Mel?"

MEL  What plot? Jeez!
*(He turns away from her)*

EDNA  *(Exasperated)*  What plot? WHAT PLOT??

MEL  *(He turns back toward her)*  The—social—economical— and—political—plot—to—undermine—the—working—classes—in —this—country.

EDNA  Oh, that plot.

MEL    Yes, *that* plot! Instead of rushing downtown every morning, stay home and listen to the radio once in a while. Listen to the talk shows. Find out what's going on in this country. Ten minutes of WQXR and you'll want to move to Switzerland.

EDNA    If it depresses you, Mel, don't listen to the talk shows. Listen to some nice music.

MEL    Nice music . . . *(laughs)* Incredible. You're a child. You're an uninformed, ignorant little child . . . They've taken it over, Edna. Our music, our culture, it's not ours any more, it's *theirs.*

EDNA    They have our music?

MEL    All of it. The arts, the media, every form of mass communication. *They got it, baby!*

EDNA    Don't get mad, Mel . . . Who?

MEL    *Who? . . . WHO??* . . . Jesus God in heaven! *Who???*

EDNA    Mel, I've got to be in the office in twenty minutes. Please tell me who's taking over so I won't be late.

MEL    All right, sit down.

EDNA    I may not get a cab, Mel. Can't you tell me who's taking over standing up?

MEL    Are you going to sit down?

EDNA    Do I have to, Mel? Is it a long name?

MEL    *Sit down, for Christ sakes!* (EDNA *sits down, while* MEL *paces)* Now . . . Once you do away with the middle class —what have you got left?

EDNA    *(She looks at him. It can't be that easy)* What's left? After you take away the middle class? (MEL *nods)* The lower class and the upper class?
        *(*MEL *stares at her incredulously)*

49

MEL  I can't talk to you. You have no understanding at all. Go on. Go to work.

EDNA  You mean there's another class besides the lower, the middle and the upper?

MEL  *(He walks to the center of the room and looks around suspiciously)*  Come here.
(EDNA *looks at him*)

EDNA  I thought you wanted me to sit down.

MEL  Will you come here. Away from the walls.
(EDNA *gets up and goes over to him in the middle of the room*)

EDNA  If it's that secret, Mel, I don't think I want to know.
*(He grabs her by the wrist and pulls her to him)*

MEL  *(In a soft voice)*  There *is* a plot, Edna. It's very complicated, very sophisticated, almost invisible . . . Maybe only a half a dozen people in this country really know about it.

EDNA  And they told it on the radio?

MEL  Yes.

EDNA  Then everyone heard it.

MEL  Did you hear it?

EDNA  No.

MEL  Then everyone didn't hear it. How many people you think listen to the radio at ten o'clock in the morning? Everybody is working. But I heard it . . . And as sure as we're standing here in the middle of the room, there is a plot going on in this country today.

EDNA  Against whom?

MEL  Against me.

EDNA  The whole country?

MEL  Not me personally. Although I'm a victim of it. A plot to change the system. To destroy the status quo. It's not just me they're after, Edna. They're after you. They're after our kids, my sisters, every one of our friends. They're after the cops, they're after the hippies, they're after the government, they're after the anarchists, they're after Women's Lib, the fags, the blacks, the whole military complex. That's who they're after, Edna.

EDNA  Who? You mentioned everyone. There's no one left.

MEL  There's someone left. Oh, baby, there's someone left all right.

EDNA  Well, I'm sure there is . . . if you say so, Mel.

MEL  *(Yells)* Don't patronize me. I know what I'm talking about. I am open to channels of information twenty-four hours a day.
*(EDNA is becoming increasingly alarmed at MEL's obvious paranoiac behavior, but doesn't quite know how to handle it yet)*

EDNA  Mel, Mel . . . Would you come here for a minute. Just sit with me for a minute. *(He sits down)* Mel . . . You know I love you and believe in you completely. I always have . . . But I just want to say something, I hope you don't misunderstand this—

MEL  You think I'm paranoiac? You think I'm having some sort of mental, nervous breakdown because I'm out of work? Because of the pressure, the strain I've been under, because I sound like a deranged person because of the personal hell I have gone through these past seven weeks. Is that it?

EDNA *(Nods)* That's it. That's exactly it, Mel . . . I wouldn't have put it that strongly, but that's more or less it. Exactly.

MEL Do you want proof, Edna? Do you want me to give you actual, indisputable proof?

EDNA *(Trying to be kinder now)* Of what, Mel?

MEL That me, that Dave Polichek, that Mike Ambrozi, Hal Chesterman, twenty-three secretaries, six point seven of the working force in this country today is unemployed not because of a recession, not because of wages and high prices, but because of a well-organized, calculated, brilliantly executed *plot!* Do you want me to give you proof right here and now in this room?

EDNA *(Hesitates)* Well—all right . . . If you want, Mel.

MEL I CAN'T GIVE YOU ANY PROOF!!! . . . *What kind of proof do I have?* I'm out of work, that's my proof . . . They won't let me work!

EDNA Who is it, Mel? Tell me who's behind the plot? Is it the kids? The addicts? The Army? The Navy? The Book-of-the-Month Club? WHO THE HELL IS IT, MEL?

MEL It is the human race! . . . It is the sudden, irrevocable deterioration of the spirit of man. It is man undermining himself, causing a self-willed, self-imposed, self-evident *self-destruction* . . . That's who it is.

EDNA *(Looks at him)* The human race? . . . The human race is responsible for the unemployment?

MEL *(A little smirk)* Surprised, aren't you?

EDNA *(Nods, quite shaken)* I never would have guessed. I kept thinking it was somebody else.

MEL *(Glares at her)* Don't mock me. Don't patronize me and don't mock me.

EDNA I'm not mocking you, Mel.

MEL *You're mocking me!* . . . I know when I'm being mocked. I know what I'm talking about. You're working, you've got a job, you're not affected by any of this.

EDNA I am so affected by it, Mel, you wouldn't believe it was possible . . .

MEL You don't know the first thing I'm talking about . . . You don't know what it is to be in my place . . . You've never stood on line for two hours waiting for an unemployment check with a shirt and tie, trying to look like you don't need the money. And some fat old dame behind the counter screaming out so everyone can hear, *"Did you look for a job this week?"* "Yes, I looked for a job." *"Did you turn down any work this week?"* "What the hell am I doing here if I turned down work this week?" . . . You never walked into your own building and had a ninety-one-year-old doorman with no teeth, asthma and beer on his breath giggle at you because *he's* working . . . You've never been on your own terrace and gotten hit with a bucket of ice-cold ice water . . . I haven't forgotten that son of a bitch! *(He goes to the terrace door, but not out on it, and yells up)* I haven't forgotten you, you son of a bitch!

EDNA Mel, don't start in again. Please don't start in again.

MEL I'm waiting for him. I'm just waiting for him. He's up there now, but one day he's gonna be down there and I'm gonna be up here and then we'll see. One cold, snowy day some son of a bitch in this building is gonna be buried under three feet of snow. They won't find him until the spring. *(Yells up again)* They won't find you until the spring, you son of a bitch!

EDNA  Mel, listen to me. Listen to me very carefully. I want you to see a doctor . . . I don't want to put it off any more, Mel, I want you to see a doctor as soon as possible. Today, Mel. Now.

MEL  *(Disregarding her, he keeps talking through her speeches)* He thinks I don't know what he looks like . . . I know what he looks like, all right . . . I know what they *all* look like. I've got their faces engraved in my brain.

EDNA  *(Going through her pocketbook)* Mel, someone gave me the name of a doctor. They say he's very good and knows about people who've gone through what you're going through . . . I'm going to call him now, Mel. I'm going to call him and make an appointment now.

MEL  *(He hasn't heard her)* They can get your clothes, Edna. They can get your clothes, your Valium, your television, your Red Label whiskey, your job, they can get everything. But they can't get your brains . . . That's my secret weapon . . . That and the snow . . . I pray to God it snows tomorrow, I'll wait for him. I bought a shovel today. Oh, yeah.

EDNA  *(Finds the number)* I'm calling him, Mel . . . I'm calling him now.
     *(She goes over to the phone. He goes over to the closet)*

MEL  Not a little shovel, a big one. The kind they use in airports . . . I'll go without shoes this winter, but I won't go without my shovel. I'll bury him so deep, they'll have to salt him out.
     *(He takes out a shovel, the bottom part of which is in a box)*

EDNA  *(At the phone)* I won't go to work this afternoon, Mel. If he's free, I'm going to take you myself . . . Don't stand near the window, Mel.
     *(She begins to dial. He opens the box and takes out a shiny new shovel)*

MEL *(A wild, joyous look on his face)* I live for it. I live for the first snow of the winter . . . He gets home at five fifteen, I checked with the doorman . . . I gave him a five-dollar tip, it was worth it. *(Yells up)* I know what time you get home, you bastard. Try using the service entrance, I got that blocked off too.

EDNA *(Into the phone)* Hello? . . . Is Doctor Frankel there, please? . . . Mrs. Edna Edison . . .

MEL *(To* EDNA, *oblivious of her on the phone)* Do you have any idea, any conception of the impact of two pounds of snow falling from a height of fourteen floors . . . They'll find him in the garage. *(Yells up)* They'll find you in the garage, you bastard . . . I know what you look like.

EDNA Hello? . . . Doctor Frankel? . . . I'm sorry to disturb you, but it's an emergency . . . No, for my husband . . . We've got to see you as soon as possible, Doctor Frankel, as soon as possible . . .

MEL *(He goes out onto the terrace)* And if it doesn't snow this winter, I'll wait till next winter . . . I'm in no hurry, smart ass. *(Yelling up)* I've got nothing but time . . . Nothing but time, baby . . .

*(He laughs. The room goes black as the curtain falls. In the darkness, the News Logo appears. We hear the voice of Roger Keating again)*

VOICE This is Roger Keating and the *Six O'Clock Report* . . . No word yet on the unsolved mugging and robbing late last night of New York State Governor Nelson Rockefeller on Sixth Avenue and Forty-eighth Street. The governor will be heard in a special interview on the *Eleven O'Clock News* from his room in Beth Israel Hospital where he is resting, which, incidentally, is entering its fifty-seventh day of the hospital strike . . . "We will not go back to work" was the cry of forty-seven municipal, state and federal judges today, defying the court order of Federal Judge Myron Ackerman. Speaking for the striking judges, Judge Mario Pecona told this to CBS reporter Bethesda Wayne.

JUDGE'S VOICE  We will not go back to woik.

GIRL'S VOICE  Judge Pecona, isn't this strike unconstitutional?

JUDGE'S VOICE  Yes, but we will not go back to woik.

GIRL'S VOICE  How do you feel about the two hundred and seventy-three people in prisons now awaiting trial?

JUDGE'S VOICE  We are underpaid. We will not go back to woik.

GIRL'S VOICE  Do you still feel this way despite the fact that President Nixon has threatened to bring in the National Guard to run the courts?

JUDGE'S VOICE  He can do what he wants, we will not go back to woik.

VOICE  The *Six O'Clock Report* will follow with a filmed story of how twenty million rats survive under the city . . . But first this message from Ultra-Brite toothpaste.
*(The News Logo fades as the curtain rises)*

*It is midafternoon, two weeks later.*

*As the curtain rises, we see three women, all in their late fif-*
*ties and dressed quite well. Two are on a sofa, one sits in arm-*
*chair. These are* MEL'S *sisters:* PAULINE, PEARL *and* JESSIE. PAU-
LINE *is doing needlepoint. Standing is* MEL'S *older brother,*
HARRY. *He wears an expensive business suit. He is looking out*
*the window. A pot of coffee and cups are on the table in front*
*of the women. They sit there silently.*

JESSIE   He was always nervous.

PEARL   Always.

JESSIE   As far back as I can remember, he was nervous.
Never sat still for a minute, always jumping up and down.
Am I lying, Pearl?

PEARL   We're his own sisters, who should know better? Up
and down, up and down . . . You want some coffee, Harry?
Take some coffee.

HARRY   I don't drink coffee.

JESSIE   He always used to fidget. Talked a mile a minute
. . . He even chewed fast—remember how fast he used to
chew?

PEARL   Wasn't I there? Didn't I see him chew? I remember
. . . Harry, why don't you take some coffee?

HARRY   When did you ever see me drink coffee? You're my
sister fifty-three years, you never saw me drink coffee.
Why would I drink coffee now?

PEARL   What do I see you, two times a year? I thought maybe
you took up coffee.

PAULINE  He wasn't nervous, he was high-strung. Melvin was high-strung.

PEARL  I call it nervous. As a baby he was nervous, as a boy he was nervous, in the Army he was nervous. How long did he last in the Army, anyway?

JESSIE  Two weeks.

PEARL  There you are. He was nervous.

PAULINE  Where do you think nerves come from? From being high-strung.

PEARL  Then why weren't any of us high-strung? We all had the same parents. He was nervous, he was fidgety, he chewed fast . . . I never saw him swallow.

JESSIE  No one could talk to him. Poppa could never talk to him, I remember.

PAULINE  How could Poppa talk to him? Mel was three years old when Poppa died.

PEARL  If he wasn't so nervous, Poppa could have talked to him.

HARRY  I never drank coffee in my life. It's poison. Goes right through the system. *(Looks toward the bedroom)* Who's she on the phone with in there anyway?

PEARL  He had the same thing in high school. A nervous breakdown. Remember when he had the nervous breakdown in high school?

HARRY  *(Turning to her)*  Who you talking about?

PEARL  Mel! He had a nervous breakdown in high school. You don't remember?

HARRY  What are you talking about? He didn't have a nervous breakdown, he had a broken arm. He fell in the gym and broke his arm.

PEARL   I'm not talking about that time.

HARRY   And once on his bicycle he broke his tooth.

PEARL   I'm not talking about that time.

HARRY   Then when are you talking about?

PEARL   I'm talking about the time he had a nervous break-down in high school. I remember it like it was yesterday, don't tell me. Pauline, tell him.

PAULINE   Mel never had a nervous breakdown.

PEARL   Isn't that funny, I thought he had a nervous break-down. Maybe I'm thinking of somebody else.

HARRY   You can't even remember that I don't drink coffee.

PAULINE   He must have had some terrible experiences in the Army.

HARRY   In two weeks? He wasn't there long enough to get a uniform. None of you know what you're talking about. There was never anything wrong with Mel. Never. His trouble was you babied him too much. All of you.

JESSIE   Why shouldn't we baby him? He was the baby, wasn't he?

HARRY   You babied him, that's his trouble. He never had the responsibilities as a child like I did. That's why he can't handle problems. That's why he flares up. He's a child, an infant.

PEARL   What if I put some milk in the coffee?

HARRY   I DON'T WANT ANY COFFEE!!

JESSIE   He doesn't want any coffee, leave him alone.

PAULINE   Correct me if I'm wrong, but when Mel was a tiny baby, didn't you think his head was too large for his body?

PEARL  Mel? Mel had a beautiful head.

PAULINE  I didn't say his head wasn't beautiful. I said it was too large for his body. It always kept falling over to one side.
*(She demonstrates)*

PEARL  *All* babies' heads fall to one side.
*(She demonstrates)*

PAULINE  I know that, but he had trouble getting his up again.
*(She demonstrates)*

HARRY  I was never babied. Poppa wouldn't allow it . . . I was never kissed from the time I was seven years old.

JESSIE  Certainly you were kissed.

HARRY  Never kissed . . . I didn't need kissing. The whole world kissed Mel, look where he is today. Who's she talking to in there all this time?

PEARL  Remember the summer he ran away?

PAULINE  He didn't run away for the whole summer. He ran away for one night.

PEARL  Who said he ran away for the whole summer?

PAULINE  Who said it? You said it. You just said, "Remember the summer he ran away?"

PEARL  So? He ran away for *one* night *one* summer.

PAULINE  But you should say it that way. Say, "Remember the summer he ran away for one night?" . . . Don't make it sound like he ran away for a whole summer. That crazy he never was.

PEARL  Did I say Mel was crazy? Who heard me mention the word crazy? Jessie, did you hear "crazy" from me?

JESSIE  I heard "crazy" but I wasn't looking where it came.

PEARL  (*To* PAULINE)  If that's what you believe, *you're* the one that's crazy.

PAULINE  All right, if it makes you happy, I'm crazy. Let me be the crazy one.

PEARL  Fine. Then it's settled. You're the crazy one.

HARRY  Listen, I've got to get back to the office, Jessie's going back to Lakewood tonight, let's try to settle things now. What are we going to do?

PAULINE  About what?

HARRY  (*Looks at her as though she's deranged*)  About *what?* About the Suez Canal. What do you mean, about what? What are we here for? What did Jessie come all the way from Lakewood for? What are we doing in that woman's house, (*Points to the bedroom*) where none of us have been invited for nine years? Our brother. Our sick brother who's had a nervous breakdown, for God's sakes.

JESSIE  (*Sniffles, wipes her eyes with a handkerchief*)  Every time I hear it—

HARRY  What are you crying *now* for? You didn't just hear. You've known for a week.

JESSIE  You think I haven't been crying the whole week? He's my brother, it hurts me.

HARRY  It hurts all of us. That's why we're here. To try to do something.

PAULINE  Harry, let her cry if she wants. She came all the way from Lakewood . . . Go on, Harry.

HARRY  Fact number one, Mel has had a nervous breakdown. Fact number two, besides a nervous breakdown, Mel doesn't have a job. The man is totally unemployed.

JESSIE *(Sniffles again)* You think that doesn't hurt me too?

PAULINE Jessie, let him finish, you can cry on the way home.

HARRY Fact—

PAULINE Go on with the facts, Harry.

HARRY Fact number three, besides a nervous breakdown and not having a job, the man is practically penniless . . . I don't want to pass any comments on how a man and a woman mishandled their money for twenty-seven years. It's none of my business how a man squandered a life's savings on bad investments for which he never asked my advice once, the kind of advice which has given me solvency, security and a beautiful summer place in the country. Thank God, *I'll* never have a nervous breakdown . . . None of that is my business. My business is what are we going to do for Mel? How much are we going to give? Somebody make a suggestion. *(The silence is deafening. No one speaks. No one looks at each other. There is a lot of coffee drinking, but no offers as to how much they're going to give . . . After what seems like an hour of silence,* HARRY *speaks again)* Well?

PEARL You're a businessman, Harry. You make a suggestion. You tell us how much we should all give.

HARRY *(Thinks a moment)* Let me have some coffee. *(*PEARL *pours him a cup of coffee)* So let's face the facts . . . The man needs help. Who else can he turn to but us? This is my suggestion. We make Mel a loan. We all chip in X number of dollars a week, and then when he gets back on his feet, when he gets straightened out, gets a job again, then he can pay us all back. That's my suggestion. What do you all think?

*(There is a moment's silence.* PAULINE *whispers to* PEARL. PEARL *nods)*

PEARL    Pauline has a question.

HARRY    What's the question?

PAULINE    How much is X number of dollars?

HARRY    X is X. We have to figure out what X is. We'll talk and we'll decide.

PAULINE    I mean is it a big X or a little x?

HARRY    It's not even an X. It's a blank until we fill X in with a figure.

PAULINE    I'm not complaining. We have to do the right thing. But when you say it like that, "X number of dollars," it sounds like a lot of money . . . I have limited capital, you know.

JESSIE    Everybody has limited capital. Nobody has *un*limited capital. Pearl, do you have unlimited capital?

PEARL    I wish I did. I'd give Mel X number of dollars in a minute.

PAULINE    All I'm asking is, how much is X. I can't figure with letters, I have to know numbers.

JESSIE    Harry, don't say X any more. We're not business-women, we don't know about X. Say a number that we can understand.

HARRY    I can't say a number until I figure out A, how much does Mel need a week, and B, how much are we willing to give. I can't even guess what X is until we figure out how much A and B come to.

PEARL    All right, suppose we figure out what A is and what

B is. And if we know that, then we'll figure what X is, right?

HARRY   Right.

PEARL   And now suppose everyone here agrees except one person. She thinks it's too much. She doesn't want to give X. She wants to give M or W, whatever. What do we do then?

HARRY   Forget X. Forget I ever said X. *(He rubs his head and drinks some more coffee)* Let's figure what Mel needs to get over his nervous breakdown . . . His biggest expense is the doctor, right? Edna says he's the best and he has to go five times a week.

PAULINE   Five times a week to the best doctor? I'm beginning to see what X is going to come to.

JESSIE   Maybe it's not even a nervous breakdown. Doctors can be wrong, too. Remember your pains last year, Pearl?

PEARL   It's true. They took out all my top teeth, then found out it was kidney stones.

HARRY   I can't believe what I'm listening to . . . You're a hundred and sixty years old between the three of you and not one of you makes any sense . . . If you'll all be quiet for a minute, I'll settle this thing.

PEARL   All right, we're quiet. Settle it, Harry.

HARRY   The most important thing is that Mel gets well, agreed?

ALL THREE   Agreed!

HARRY   And that the only way he's going to get well is to see a doctor. Agreed?

ALL THREE   Agreed.

HARRY   And it is our obligation, as his only living relatives

—not counting his wife, no disrespect intended—to bear the financial responsibility of that burden. Agreed?

ALL THREE  Agreed.

HARRY  And we'll all see this thing through to the end whether it takes a week or a month or a year or even five years. Agreed? *(There is stony silence)* Okay. Our first disagreement.

PAULINE  No one's disagreeing. We're all in agreement. Except when you mention things like five years. I don't see any sense in curing Mel and ending up in the poorhouse. If, God forbid, that happened, would he be in any position to help us? He's not too able to begin with.

JESSIE  So what should we do, Harry? You know how to figure these things. What should we do?

HARRY  Well, obviously we can't afford to let Mel be sick forever. We've got to put a time limit on it. Agreed?

ALL THREE  Agreed.

HARRY  What do we give him to get better? Six months?

PAULINE  It shouldn't take six months. If that doctor's as good as Edna says, it shouldn't take six months.
  *(The door to the bedroom is heard closing)*

PEARL  Shhh . . . She's coming.

PAULINE  We'll let Harry do the talking.

PEARL  And then we'll settle everything. Thank God, it's almost over.
  *(They all assume a pose of innocence and calm. EDNA comes out of the bedroom)*

EDNA  I'm sorry I was so long. I was just talking to Doctor Frankel. Mel's on his way home, he'll be here in a minute.

HARRY  How is Mel? What does the doctor say?

EDNA Well, it's hard to tell. Mel is having a very rough time. He's in a very depressed state, he's not himself. He's completely withdrawn. He sits in that chair sometimes for hours without saying a word. You'll see when he comes in, he's a different person.

JESSIE *(Wipes her eyes with a hanky, sniffs)* It hurts me every time I hear it . . .

PAULINE So what is it, a nervous breakdown? Is it a nervous breakdown? You can tell us. We're his family. It's a nervous breakdown, isn't it?

EDNA Yes, in a way I guess you can say it's a nervous breakdown.

PEARL I knew it, I knew it. He had the same thing in high school.

HARRY So what's the diagnosis? What does the doctor say?

EDNA *(Shrugs)* Mel needs care and treatment. He's a very good doctor, he thinks Mel's going to be all right, but it's just going to take time.

PAULINE How much time? A month? Two months? More than two months?

EDNA He can't tell yet.

PAULINE He can guess, can't he? Three months? Four months? More than four months?

EDNA There's no way of telling yet, Pauline. It could be a month, it could be two months, it could be two *years.*

PAULINE No, two years is out of the question. I refuse to go along with two years.

EDNA I'm not saying it will be. I'm just saying we don't know yet.

HARRY   Can I say something? Can I get a word in?

PAULINE   *(Turning away from* EDNA*)*   I wish you would say something, Harry. I wish you would do the talking.

HARRY   Thank you very much.

PAULINE   Because two years is ridiculous.

PEARL   Go on, Harry.

HARRY   We're all very concerned, Edna. Very concerned. After all, he's our brother.

JESSIE   Since he was a baby.

HARRY   Can I please do the talking?

PEARL   Will you let him do the talking, Jessie? . . . Go on, Harry.

HARRY   We're very concerned. We appreciate that you're his wife, you're going to do all you can, but we know it's not going to be enough. We want to help. We've talked it out among ourselves and . . . we're prepared to take over the financial burden of the doctor. You take care of the apartment, the food, the miscellaneous, we'll pay the doctor bills. Whatever they come to.

EDNA   I'm . . . I'm overwhelmed . . . I'll be very truthful with you, I never expected that . . . I am deeply touched and overwhelmed. I don't know what to say . . .

HARRY   You don't have to say anything.

PAULINE   Just tell us what you think the bills will come to.

EDNA   That's very generous of you all, but I couldn't let you do that. Mel wouldn't let me do it.

HARRY   Don't be ridiculous. Where you going to get the money from, a bank? You can't put up a nervous breakdown as collateral.

67

EDNA  I have no idea how long Mel will be in treatment. It could run into a fortune.

HARRY  Let us worry about that. The money, we'll take care of.

EDNA  But it could run as high as twenty, twenty-five thousand dollars.
*(There is a long pause. The sisters all look at HARRY)*

PAULINE  Harry, can I say something to you in private?

HARRY  We don't need any private discussions.

PAULINE  We just found out what X is . . . Don't you think we ought to discuss X a little further?

HARRY  It's not necessary. I don't care what it's going to cost. The three of you can contribute whatever you think you can afford, *I'll* make up the deficit . . . If it's fifteen, if it's twenty, if it's twenty-five thousand, I'll see that it's taken care of, as long as Mel has the best medical treatment . . . That's all I have to say.
*(He nods his head as though taking a little bow)*

EDNA  *(Moved)*  I'm—I'm speechless . . . What do I say?

HARRY  You don't say nothing.

PEARL  We just want to do the right thing.

EDNA  I know none of us have been very close the last few years.

PAULINE  Nine. Nine years was the last time we were invited.

EDNA  Has it been that long? I suppose it's been my fault. Maybe I haven't tried to understand you. Maybe you haven't tried to understand me. Anyway, I appreciate it more than you can imagine, but we really don't need it.

HARRY  What are you talking about? Certainly you need it.

EDNA  Over the years, we've managed to save something. I have some jewelry I can sell . . .

HARRY  You're not going to sell your jewelry.

PAULINE  Maybe she doesn't wear it any more. Let the woman talk.

EDNA  Mel can cash in his insurance policy and I have my job. I can manage whatever the medical expenses come to, but if you really want to help . . . What I'm worried about is Mel's future.

JESSIE  We all are, darling.

EDNA  It's not easy for a man of Mel's age to get a job today, to start all over again . . .

HARRY  If he knew lighting fixtures, I would take him in a minute.

PEARL  Certainly, my God.

EDNA  If he could just get out of New York and move to the country somewhere, he would be a hundred per cent better off.

HARRY  I agree a thousand per cent.

EDNA  I was thinking of a summer camp. Mel is wonderful with children and sports, I could do the cooking, the girls will help out, we can hire a small staff . . . There's a lovely place in Vermont that's for sale. We could have it for next summer. Don't you think Mel would be better off there?

HARRY  Again, a thousand per cent.

EDNA  They want twenty-five thousand dollars down in cash . . . So instead of giving it to us for the doctor, would you lend it to us for the camp?

(*There is a hush, a definite hush.* HARRY *looks at* EDNA *in disbelief*)

69

HARRY  A summer camp? . . . Twenty-five thousand dollars for a summer camp?

EDNA  The price is a hundred thousand. But they want twenty-five thousand down.

HARRY  *A hundred thousand dollars* for a *summer camp??* . . . Run by a man with a nervous breakdown?

EDNA  He'll be all right by next summer.

HARRY  Do you know what it is for a *normal* person to be responsible for that many boys and girls? The lawsuits you're open for?

EDNA  I don't understand. You were willing to give Mel the money for a doctor. Why won't you lend it to him for a camp?

HARRY  Because with a camp you can go broke. With a doctor you can go broke too, but you get better.

EDNA  All right. *You* pay for the doctor. *I'll* invest in the camp.

HARRY  You mean we should pay to get Mel healthy so you can lose your money in a camp and get him sick again? . . . Then you'll come to us for more money for another doctor?

EDNA  I thought you wanted to do something. I thought you wanted to help him.

HARRY  We *do* want to help him.

EDNA  *Then help him!*

HARRY  Not when he's sick. When he's better, we'll help him.

EDNA  *(Turns to the sisters)*  Is that how the rest of you feel? Do you all agree with Harry?
   *(They all look at one another uncomfortably)*

PAULINE *(Looking in her coffee cup)* I am not familiar with Vermont.

JESSIE I'd say yes in a minute, but Harry's the spokesman.

PEARL I'd have to go up and see it first, but I can't travel with my leg.

EDNA All right . . . Forget it. Forget the money, we don't need it. We'll get along without it very nicely, thank you . . . I'm surprised you even offered it . . . It's good to know that the minute Mel is completely recovered and back on his own two strong feet again, I can count on you for help. That's just when we'll need it. *(She starts toward the bedroom)* Will you please excuse me? I've got to make some calls before I go back to the office . . . Just in case I don't see any of you for another nine years, *(Points to the tray)* have some cookies . . .
   *(She storms into the bedroom, slamming the door behind her. They all look at one another, stunned)*

HARRY What did I say that was wrong? You're my witnesses, what did I say that was wrong?

PEARL You said nothing wrong. I'm a witness.

PAULINE The truth is, she doesn't *want* us to help him. She's jealous. And I was willing to give him *anything*.

JESSIE *(To PEARL)* Does that mean we're not giving for the doctor either?

PEARL *(To JESSIE)* Why don't you pay attention? You never pay attention.

HARRY A man in his condition running a summer camp. I spoke to him on the phone Thursday, he could hardly say hello.

PAULINE Why does she hate us? What did we ever do to her? It's jealousy, that's what it is.

PEARL  That's all it is.

PAULINE  Jealousy . . . I'd like to get him out of here. He could move in with me, I'd love to take care of him.

HARRY  A man in his condition running a summer camp. It would take him until August to figure out how to blow up the volleyball.

JESSIE  If nothing is settled yet, can I give my vote to Pauline? I've got shopping to do.

HARRY  *Sit down! Nothing has been settled!* . . . We'll have to settle it with Mel.

PEARL  With Mel? How can Mel make a decision in his condition?

HARRY  Him I can reason with. He's only had a nervous breakdown. *That* woman is crazy! Let me have some more coffee.

(PEARL *starts to pour* HARRY *some more coffee when suddenly we hear a key in the latch and the door opens.* MEL *enters. He looks aged. Perhaps aged isn't the right word. Distant might describe it better. His eyes are ringed and his hair is slightly unkempt; he has a glazed expression on his face. He opens the door and closes it, puts his key in his pocket, and goes across the room and into the kitchen without looking up and without noticing the others sitting there. They all look at him, puzzled and slightly horrified at his behavior. In the kitchen* MEL *pours himself a glass of water and then takes out a small vial of pills. He takes a pill, places it in his mouth and drinks the water. He comes back into the living room. He doesn't seem startled or surprised; it is as though he were sixteen again and coming into a familiar setting. When he speaks, his voice lacks emotion)*

MEL  I just had a nice walk.

HARRY *(Goes to him)* Hello, Mel.

MEL *(Looks at him)* From Eighty-second and Park. *(He whispers)* Don't tell Edna. She doesn't like me to walk too far.

HARRY Mel? *(Points to himself)* Do you know who this is?

MEL What do you mean, Harry?

HARRY Nothing. Nothing. *(Points to the girls)* Look who's here to see you, Mel.
    *(MEL turns and looks at the sisters)*

MEL *(Smiles)* Why shouldn't they come to see me? They're my own sisters, aren't they? Who has better sisters than I have? *(He opens up his arms to greet them and goes to PAULINE)* Pauline! How are you?
    *(He kisses her. She hugs him)*

PAULINE Mel, darling.

MEL *(Turns to JESSIE)* And Jessie. Sweet Jessica Jessie . . .
    *(He kisses her)*

JESSIE You look—wonderful, Mel.
    *(She sniffles and fights back the tears. His back is to PEARL)*

MEL Everyone's here but Pearl.

PEARL *(How could he miss her?)* Here I am, Mel.

MEL *(Turns around)* There she is, hiding . . . Always hiding from your baby brother.

PEARL I wasn't hiding, Mel. I was just sitting.

HARRY *(Takes MEL by the arm)* Mel, sit down. We want to talk to you.

MEL *(Looks at him suspiciously)* Something is wrong. Someone in the family is sick.

HARRY   No. No one is sick, Mel . . . Everybody is fine. Sit down.
*(He urges* MEL *into a chair.* MEL *sits down)*

MEL   I had such a nice walk.

JESSIE   Isn't that wonderful, Mel. You always used to like to walk.
*(*PEARL *gets up and goes over to the window behind* MEL. *She takes out a hanky and wipes her eyes)*

MEL   Remember how I used to like to walk, Jessie?

JESSIE   I do, Mel, I was just saying that.

PAULINE   You're looking very well, darling.

MEL   Thank you, Pauline.

PAULINE   Are you feeling all right?
*(She swallows the last word)*

MEL   What's that, darling?

PAULINE   I said, are you feeling all right?

MEL   Am I feeling all right? . . . Yes . . . Yes, I just had a very nice walk.

PAULINE   Oh, that's nice, dear.

MEL *(Looks around)*   Where's Pearl? Did Pearl go home?

PEARL *(At the window, behind him)*   Here I am, Mel. I didn't go home.

MEL *(Turns around)*   There she is. Hiding again . . . She always used to hide from me.

HARRY *(Pacing)*   Mel . . .

MEL   Yes, Harry?

HARRY *(Stops)*   Mel . . .

PEARL  Harry wants to say something to you, Mel.

MEL  What is it, Harry?

HARRY  Nothing, Mel . . . Nothing.

MEL  You don't look well to me, Harry. You're working too hard . . . Don't work so hard, Harry.

HARRY  I won't, Mel.

MEL  You have to relax more. Three things I learned at the doctor's, Harry. You have to relax, you mustn't take the world too seriously . . . and you have to be very careful of what you say when you go out on the terrace.
    *(Curtain. News Logo in—Six O'Clock Report)*

VOICE OVER  This is the *Six O'Clock Report* with Stan Jennings sitting in for Roger Keating, who was beaten and mugged last night outside our studio following the *Six O'Clock Report* . . . A Polish freighter, the six-thousand-ton *Majorska,* sailed into New York harbor in dense fog at 7.00 A.M. this morning and crashed into the Statue of Liberty. Two seamen were injured and electrical damage caused flickering in Miss Liberty's torch. It was the first recorded maritime accident involving the famed statue, although the Polish freighter had been in six previous sea collisions . . . And today, in a midtown hotel following a convention of the National Psychiatric Society, seventeen of the leading psychiatrists in the United States were trapped between floors in an elevator for over forty-five minutes. Panic broke out and twelve of the doctors were treated for hysteria.

*It is mid-December, six weeks later. It is late afternoon.*

*As the curtain rises,* EDNA *is on the phone. She is wearing a winter coat over her suit. A grocery package is in her arms. She has obviously just come in and seems rather distraught.*

EDNA *(Into the phone)* Hello? . . . Is the superintendent there, please? . . . Mrs. Edison. 14A. I have no water. There is no water in the house . . . What do you mean he's out? Out where? I have no water. I just walked in the house . . . Well, if they're fixing the pipes, shouldn't he be in the building? He's getting paid for that, isn't he? . . . I didn't see any sign in the elevator. I have other things on my mind besides reading signs in elevators . . . I have no electricity in the kitchen . . . No, just the kitchen . . . Just—the—kitchen! I don't know why, I'm not an electrician . . . I can't wait until seven o'clock . . . My food is spoiling and you're telling me your husband is out? . . . I don't blame him. I wouldn't hang around this building either if I didn't have to. *(MEL has entered from the front door during the phone conversation. She hangs up and stands there)* There's no water. The water is shut off . . . They're fixing the pipes, we won't have any until five, six, seven, they're not sure when . . . And there's no electricity in the kitchen. The refrigerator's off . . . I called the super, he's out.

> *(She sits down. He goes to the table and puts his paints back in their box. His easel and canvas are left standing)*

MEL  I'm not going back. I'm not going back to that doctor. He's a quack. He sits there cleaning his pipe, playing with his watch fob, and doesn't know what the hell he's talking about. The man is a quack. If I'm getting better, I'm doing it myself . . . I'm working my *own* problems out. That man sits there playing with a pipe scooper watching *me* get better for forty dollars an hour . . . I got mirrors in the house, I can watch myself get better. I could lay there for fifty minutes, if I don't say a word, he won't say a word. What would kill him *(During this, he has been going to the closet, putting his paint box, easel and canvas away)* to ask me a question? "What's wrong, Mr. Edison? What are you thinking about?" . . . Not him. If I don't bring it up, he don't ask. I'm curing myself, I'm telling you. I see how you look when you come home every night. Killing yourself, breaking your back and for what? To give forty dollars an hour to a pipe cleaner? I can't take it any more, Edna. I can't see you turning yourself into an old woman just for me. What's the point in it? As soon as I'm all right again, I'll be too young for you.

EDNA  *(Holding back tears)*  Well, I don't think you have to worry about that any more, Mel . . . We went out of business today.

MEL  Who did?

EDNA  We did. The business that I'm in is out of business. There is no business in that place any more.

MEL  They let you go?

EDNA  If *they're* not staying, what do they need me for?

MEL  You mean completely out of business?

EDNA  They went bankrupt. They overextended themselves. One of the partners may go to jail.
      *(She starts to cry)*

MEL  You don't go bankrupt overnight. You must have had some inkling.

EDNA *(Crying)* I had *no* inkling . . . I did, but I was afraid to think about it . . . What's happening, Mel? Is the whole world going out of business?

MEL *(Goes over to her)* Okay. It's all right, Edna, it's all right.

EDNA *(Sobbing)* I thought we were such a strong country, Mel. If you can't depend on America, who can you depend on?

MEL Ourselves, Edna. We have to depend on each other.

EDNA I don't understand how a big place like that can just go out of business. It's not a little candy store. It's a big building. It's got stone and marble with gargoyles on the roof. Beautifully hand-chiseled gargoyles, Mel. A hundred years old. They'll come tomorrow with a sledgehammer and kill the gargoyles.

MEL It's just a job, Edna. It's not your whole life.

EDNA You know what I thought about on the way home? One thing. I only had one thing on my mind . . . A bath. A nice, hot bath. *(Sobs again)* And now the water went out of business.

MEL It'll come back on. Everything is going to come back on, Edna. They're not going to shut us off forever.

EDNA *(She yells)* I want my bath! I want my water! Tell them I want my bath, Mel!

MEL It's off, Edna. What can I do? There's nothing I can do.

EDNA *(Yells)* Bang on the pipes. Tell them there's a woman upstairs who needs an emergency bath. If I don't sit in some water, Mel, I'm going to go crazy. Bang on the pipes.

MEL   Edna, be reasonable . . .

EDNA   *(Screams)   I banged for you, why won't you bang for me?*

MEL   Shh, it's all right, baby. It's all right.

EDNA   *(Still sobbing)*   It's *not*. It's *not* all right. Why are you saying it's all right? Are you out of your mind? Oh, God, Mel, I'm sorry. I didn't mean that. Please forgive me, Mel.

MEL   It's all right, Edna . . . Please calm down.

EDNA   I don't know what I'm saying any more. It's too much for me, Mel. I have no strength left, Mel. Nothing. I couldn't open my pocketbook on the bus; a little boy had to help me.

MEL   Of course you have strength.

EDNA   I have anger, no strength . . . If something happens to me, Mel, who's going to take care of us?

MEL   I am. I always took care of you, didn't I?

EDNA   But who's going to take care of us now, Mel?

MEL   Me, Edna. Me!

EDNA   You, Mel?

MEL   Don't you trust me, Edna? Don't you believe in me any more?

EDNA   Let's leave, Mel. Let's give up and leave . . . Let them have it. Let them have their city . . . Let them keep their garbage and their crooks and their jobs and their broken gargoyles . . . I just want to live out the rest of my life with you and see my girls grow up healthy and happy and once in a while I would like to have some water and take a bath . . . Please, Mel . . . Please.

MEL   All right, Edna . . . We'll go . . . We'll go.
*(The doorbell chimes)*

EDNA *(Yells)*   That's the super!

MEL   I'll take care of it! Edna, you're very upset. Why don't you relax, and wait in the tub for the water to come on . . .

EDNA   All right, Mel . . . I'm sorry if I upset you.
*(She turns and goes off into the bedroom. He turns, goes over to the door and opens it. HARRY stands there; he is carrying an attaché case)*

HARRY   Hello, Mel . . . All right if I come in?

MEL *(Surprised)*   Sure, Harry, sure. I didn't know you were in New York.

HARRY *(Speaks softly)*   I had some business, and besides, I wanted to talk to you. How you feeling? All right?

MEL   Don't be so solemn, Harry. It's not a hospital room. I'm all right.
*(HARRY enters; MEL closes the door)*

HARRY   I brought you some apples from the country. *(He opens his attaché case)* Wait'll you taste these. *(He takes some apples from the case)* You always loved apples, I remember . . . Are you allowed to eat them now?

MEL   Apples don't affect the mind, Harry. They're not going to drive me crazy. Thank you. That's very nice of you.

HARRY   Is Edna here?

MEL   Yeah, she's in the tub. She's not feeling very well.

HARRY   It's all right. She doesn't want to see me. I understand.

MEL  It's not that, Harry. She's very tired.

HARRY  The woman doesn't like me. It's all right. The whole world can't love you . . . I feel badly that it's my brother's wife, but that's what makes horse racing. I'm only staying two minutes. I wanted to deliver this in person and then I'll go.

MEL  You came eight miles to bring me six apples? Harry, that's very sweet but it wasn't necessary.

HARRY  Not the apples, Mel. I have something a little more substantial than apples. *(Reaches in his pocket and takes out a check)* Here. This is for you and Edna . . . The apples are separate.
    (MEL *takes the check and looks at it*)

MEL  What's this?

HARRY  It's a check. It's the money. Go buy yourself a summer camp. *(Good-naturedly)* Go. July and August, take care of six hundred running noses. Have a good time.
    *(He gets up to go)*

MEL  Harry, this is twenty-five thousand dollars.

HARRY  Your sisters and I contributed equally, fifty-fifty. I'm telling them about it tomorrow.

MEL  I don't understand.

HARRY  I don't understand myself. Why would anyone want to run a summer camp? But if that gives you pleasure, then this gives me pleasure . . .

MEL  When did Edna ask you for this?

HARRY  What's the difference? It's over. Everybody got a little excited. Everyone was trying to do the right thing. Take the money, buy your crazy camp.

MEL  Harry!

HARRY  Yes?

MEL  In the first place . . . thank you. In the second place, I can't take it.

HARRY  Don't start in with me. It took me six weeks to decide to give it to you.

MEL  I can't explain it to you, Harry. But I just can't take the money.

HARRY  Why don't you let me do this for you? Why won't you let me have the satisfaction of making you happy?

MEL  You already have, by offering it. Now make me happier by tearing it up. They see this much money in this neighborhood, you'll never make it to your car.

HARRY  You let everyone else do things for you. You let everyone else take care of you. Edna, Pearl. Pauline, Jessie. Everybody but me, your brother. Why am I always excluded from the family?

MEL  They're three middle-aged widows, they're looking for someone to take care of. I made them a present, I got sick. What do you want from me, Harry?

HARRY  I had to work when I was thirteen years old. I didn't have time to be the favorite.

MEL  Harry, let's not go into that again. You want to be the favorite, I give it to you. I'll call the girls up tonight and tell them from now on, you're the favorite.

HARRY  I'm not blaming you! I'm not blaming you. It's only natural. If there are two brothers in the family and one is out working all day, the one who stays home is the favorite.

MEL  Harry, I don't want to seem impolite. But Edna's not feeling well, we have no water, and all our food is defrosting. I'm really not in the mood to discuss why you're not the favorite.

HARRY  I lived in that house for thirty-one years, not once did anyone ever sing me "Happy Birthday."

MEL  *(Exasperated)*  Not true, Harry. You always had a birthday party. You always had a big cake.

HARRY  I had parties, I had cakes, no one ever sang "Happy Birthday."

MEL  All right, this year I'm going to hire a big chorus, Harry, and we're going to sing you "Happy Birthday."

HARRY  Eleven years old I was wearing long pants. Fourteen I had a little mustache . . . At the movies I had to bring my birth certificate, they wanted to charge me adult prices.

MEL  I know, Harry. You grew up very fast.

HARRY  Did you ever see Pearl's family album? There are no pictures of me as a boy. I skipped right over it. Thousands of pictures of you on bicycles, on ponies, in barber chairs . . . one picture of me in a 1938 Buick. I looked like Herbert Hoover.

MEL  I'm sorry, Harry.

HARRY  I'm going to tell you something now, Mel. I never told this to anybody. I don't think you've got a brain for business. I don't think you know how to handle money. I don't think you can handle emotional problems. I think you're a child. A baby. A spoiled infant . . . And as God is my judge, many's the night I lay in bed envying you . . . Isn't that something? For a man in my position to

envy a man in your position? . . . Isn't that something?
What I have, you'll never have . . . But what you've got,
I'd like to have just once—just for an hour to see what it
feels like to be the favorite.

MEL  What if I gave you a big kiss right on the mouth?

HARRY  You kiss me, I'll break every bone in your body
. . . I'll call you. Listen, forget what I said. I changed my
mind. I don't want to be the favorite. Not if I have to be
kissed by Jessie and Pauline.

MEL  Try it, you might like it.

HARRY  I tried it, I didn't like it . . . What if I lent you twelve
thousand? You start a small camp. Five boys, two girls.

MEL  How about a little kiss on the cheek?

HARRY  You're not better yet. I don't care what your doctor
says, you've not better yet.
    *(He leaves, closing the door behind him)*

MEL  Edna! . . . *EDNA!*
    *(She comes out, wearing a bathrobe)*

EDNA  What is it, Mel? What is it?

MEL  *(He paces angrily, trying to find the right words, as she
stands there waiting)*  You asked Harry? You asked my
family for twenty-five thousand dollars for a summer camp?

EDNA  I didn't ask . . . They offered the money for a doctor
. . . I told them I didn't need it for a doctor, I needed it
for a camp.

MEL  Don't you see how humiliating it is for me to ask my
family for money? Don't you see that?

EDNA  You didn't ask them. You weren't the one who was
humiliated. *I was!* I was the one who sat here in front of

the Spanish Inquisition. You were out taking a nice *tranquilized walk in the park.*

MEL    Tranquilized? Tranquilized? . . . I was sedated, Edna, not tranquilized. SEDATED!

EDNA    I don't care if you were petrified! I was the one who was humiliated . . . Next time *you* be humiliated and *I'll* be sedated!

MEL    *(Really loud)*   You realize you're talking to a man who just had a nervous breakdown? Don't you have any regard for a man's illness?

EDNA    *(Yelling back)*   You don't sound sick to me now. You sound like you *always* sound!

MEL    I'm not talking about *now*, I'm talking about *then!* I was sedated, Edna, not tranquilized. SEDATED!

EDNA    *(Yells)*   Well, I wish to God you'd get sedated again so you'd stop yelling at me.

WOMAN'S VOICE    *(From above)*   Will you shut up down there, you hoodlums!

EDNA    *(Rushes out onto the terrace, yells up)*   Who are you calling hoodlums?

WOMAN'S VOICE    You and your loud-mouthed husband.

EDNA    *(Yells up)*   Don't you call us names. Your husband isn't half the man my husband is. We haven't forgotten the water. We remember the water.
           *(MEL goes out onto the terrace)*

WOMAN'S VOICE    My husband'll be home in an hour. If you don't shut up down there, you're gonna get more of the same.

EDNA  Ha! With what! Where are you gonna get the water? Where's your water, big mouth!?

MEL  *(Pulling her away)*  Edna, get away from there. *(He is out on the terrace now and calls up)* I'm sorry. My wife didn't mean to yell. We were just discus—*(He gets hit with the pail of water. He reenters the room—drenched)* They did it again . . .
   *(He sits down)*

EDNA  *(Sitting, bewildered)*  Where did they get the water? . . . Where did they get the water?

MEL  People like that always have water . . . They save it so that people like us can always get it.
   *(They are both seated . . . There is silence for a few moments)*

EDNA  *(Looks at him)*  I think you've behaving very well, Mel. I think you're taking it beautifully this time . . . That shows real progress, Mel. I think you've *grown* through this experience, Mel, I really do. *(And suddenly, behind them on the terrace, we see it begin to snow)* Maybe you're right. Maybe you really *don't* have to go back to the doctor any more . . . I'm so proud of you, Mel, so proud . . . Because you're better than them . . . Better than all of them, Mel . . .
   *(Snow falls—slowly at first, but steadily increasing. MEL, sensing something, turns and looks behind him. EDNA looks at MEL, then turns to look at the terrace to see what MEL is looking at. She sees the snow. They look at each other, then turn back and look at the snow again. MEL looks at his watch. He looks at the snow once more, then turns and slowly gets up and goes over to the closet. EDNA watches him. He opens the closet door and gets out his shovel. He looks at the snow once more, looks at his watch, then goes back and sits in his chair, one hand holding his shovel, the other around EDNA's shoulder,*

*a contemporary* American Gothic. *Then we hear the voice of* ROGER KEATING)

ROGER KEATING  This is Roger Keating and the *Six O'Clock Report* . . . Heavy snow warnings have been posted along the eastern seaboard tonight, and here in New York a record forty-three inches have been forecast . . . Snow plows were ordered out on the streets and city residents were asked to get out their shovels in a joint effort to show how New Yorkers can live together and work together in a common cause.

Curtain

## ABOUT THE AUTHOR

Since 1960, a Broadway season without a NEIL SIMON comedy or musical has been a rare one. During Broadway's 1966–67 season, *Barefoot in the Park*, *The Odd Couple*, *Sweet Charity*, and *Star-Spangled Girl* were all running simultaneously; in the 1970–71 season, Broadway theatergoers had their choice of *Plaza Suite*, *Last of the Red Hot Lovers*, and *Promises, Promises*. Mr. Simon began his writing career in television and has now distinguished himself as a playwright by producing ten successful Broadway comedies in a row. He has also written for the screen, successfully adapting *Barefoot in the Park* and *The Odd Couple*, and has also written an original screenplay, *The Out-of-Towners*, which starred Jack Lemmon and Sandy Dennis.

By his own analysis, "Doc" Simon has always been "that person sitting in the corner who's observing it all" for all of his forty-four years, an insight he explores in his introduction entitled "Portrait of the Artist as a Schizophrenic" written for the anthology of his plays published by Random House in 1971. That volume, *The Comedy of Neil Simon*, is a tribute to the brilliance of its author, as are the Tony Award he received as best playwright of 1965, and his selection as *Cue* magazine's Entertainer of the Year for 1972. Mr. Simon lives in New York City with his wife and two daughters.